FOOD WASTE PHILOSOPHY

FOOD WASTE
PHILOSOPHY

Shane Jordan

SilverWood

Published in 2015 by SilverWood Books

SilverWood Books Ltd
14 Small Street, Bristol, BS1 1DE, United Kingdom
www.silverwoodbooks.co.uk

ISBN 978-1-78132-042-6

British Library Cataloguing in Publication Data
A CIP catalogue record for this book is available
from the British Library

Set in Baskerville MT and Futura by SilverWood Books Ltd
Printed on responsibly sourced paper

Note for Readers

The ideas expressed within *Food Waste Philosophy* are based on the individual opinion of the author. The author makes no representations as to the accuracy or completeness of any information and the reader should exercise caution when cooking with food waste.

Contents

Food Waste Philosophy

Introduction   11

Is There Such a Thing as Food Waste?   14

Food Waste in the UK   16

How I See Food   22

Am I a Cook?   24

Bristol, More Than Just a Bridge   35

My Time at FoodCycle   41

Real People, Real Words   46

Vegetarianism vs. Vegan vs. Meat Eaters   51

Education   56

Make the Most of Leftovers   61

Health   63

I Can't Cook...   68

Food Waste Recipes

Pizza Crostini   77

Tudor Salad   78

Mediterranean Spicy Omelette   79

Banana Skin Curry   80

Bread Batons With Thai Chilli Sauce   82

Spanish Cheese on Toast   83

Sweet French Domitille   84

Curried Pancakes   85

Winter Wicca Pie   86

Child's Play   88

Coconut Island Cakes   89

Final Thoughts   90

Bibliography   93

Acknowledgements   94

FOOD WSTE PHILOSOPHY

Introduction

I'm a vegetarian chef from Bristol and I started cooking when I was asked to volunteer on a veggie food stall in Broadmead and the Harbourside. It was then that I introduced my curried pancakes and Jamaican patties to the public. They liked what I did so much that I continued to help and promote the positive aspects of a veggie diet.

After I finished with food stalls, I started working at Kabele Café in Easton where I had the chance to experiment with food and try new recipes – most of which proved very successful. Once my reputation had been built, I started to help with events such as Taunton Vegan Food Fair, Bristol Vegan Fayre, and Bristol and Brighton's Vegfest UK.

I enjoyed cooking but I always wanted to test myself, so I went in search of a new approach. A friend took me to lunch at Easton Community Centre where I saw volunteers from Bristol University cooking meals for the community. I wanted to help, and they told me that their philosophy of cooking was based on the use of surplus food. I became fascinated. These fascinations led me to join the team, who called themselves FoodCycle. They took surplus food from local businesses and made community meals to reduce food waste. In a few months, I became cooking manager and led teams of volunteers to cook for the community. While doing that, I helped a climate change movement called Green Vision, assisted their chef with cooking, and helped with information stalls in Green Park Station. I worked in the Arc Café, before it closed, where I came up with my famous 'banana skin curry', and started doing work in schools. I teamed up with Natural Balance Foods, a young British health food retailer, and gave talks and dished out food samples to local schools, enabling me to get feedback from the children about the issues they have with food and encourage them to try different things and question their way of living. A big highlight was cooking for The Julian Trust two years running, first as an assistant chef and the second year as a head chef. Cooking for lots of people, running a team, and making food for people who really need it are my best memories to date.

I have also worked with Bath and North East Somerset Council's waste awareness officers to assist with their philosophy on recycling food waste and keeping their city clean. I'm dedicated to helping improve the cities of Bristol and Bath, and look forward to bigger projects – perhaps in London. No matter what the future holds, I will continue to do my part to help reduce food waste, promote a veggie diet, and educate people about cooking skills. In addition, I aim to do more sustainable things such as creating eco-friendly provisions for children that reduce cost and expand natural resources, helping to plant new trees in parks to aid natural wildlife, and continuing to learn and progress as a human being. I feel life is about contributing something that will last. The quotes of others through history have inspired me, and I hope to do the same one day. In the end, I want to look back and know that I contributed to environmental sustainability; that I used my creative ability to build a foundation of positivity, helping people as well as wildlife to flourish and grow.

About the title: the book's called *Food Waste Philosophy* because it's about my thoughts on food and waste; how I see things, my experiences, and how collectively we can do a lot more than people may think. Hopefully, by sharing my experiences with food and people, I can help you reflect on what you do and see things from a different perspective. I am constantly learning new things, so I'm sure by the time you have finished this book, I will have learned something new that I wish I had put in here, or something I may put in another book.

Why Write This Book?

Well, it all comes down to voicing my views; giving myself the opportunity to speak to the public, and allowing people to know who I am and what I stand for. I've been vegetarian for five years now, been to many different cities and towns throughout the UK, and have acquired a lot of formal and informal knowledge on food, food waste and vegetarianism. Yet I see so many issues that need to be raised. There are so many things that need to be said but people are either too scared, or don't bother, or don't realise. I don't want to preach, just to give my opinion on things to do with food waste, vegetarianism and community cohesion. What I mean by this is coming together as a community. Celebrating our different cultures and being one city, instead of being single isolated groups. I believe the best books are objective, thought-provoking ones that allow you to contemplate what has been said, and make you want to read them again.

In addition, this book serves as an example of someone having the confidence to give their all to something they feel passionate about, and to let others know through a book. It can be very scary to let others judge you, your thoughts, feelings and beliefs, but it can also hit positive nerves that allow others to recognise and resonate with you too. Some people say, "I've always wanted to write a book" but they don't actually write it. This is my book, my views, written by Shane Jordan. It's about expressing the way I feel and really opening up. I see this book being more than just about food waste, but about community, cooking skills, and dietary knowledge. It's not a book just for vegetarians, not just academics, students or families, but also a book for anyone interested in food. I hold views but not an ideology, because any recipe can be turned into a meat dish. Most of my recipes are inspired by books of meat and vegetarian dishes.

Hopefully, this book will give you something to think about, help you save some money on your shopping bill, and give you some know-how on certain things. If I'm able to do that then my mission is fulfilled: a book that is useful to have in the kitchen and out, and provides a good read. I hope you enjoy reading about me and my views, and making some of my recipes.

Is There Such a Thing as Food Waste?

What is waste? Is it something that has no use? When I was young, I was taught to throw unwanted food in the bin if I had finished with it. I would scrape the leftovers into the general bin with everything else and that was that – all gone. Back then, recycling or composting had not even been heard of. Other friends did the same too, and the teachers, so it was the norm. Outside, I would throw food on the floor with total disregard for littering. I used to say, "The bin man's job is to pick up my rubbish, so I'm giving him something to do."

When I was cooking at school, I was taught to cut away the 'bad' parts and cook with the 'good' parts. Is there really such a thing as a 'good' part or 'bad' part? I raise my eyebrows now when I think of those naughty teachers telling me things like that! These things became the norm for me and others around me. Television showed the same. I would watch Yan Can Cook, MasterChef and Delia Smith on TV. I would see a division between food and waste. We are all conditioned never to see them as the same.

Even as an adult now, I am so surprised that food is still seen this way. If food is the base for survival, whether cooked or uncooked, and we choose not to use some of it, is it waste? I see food as a resource: something that can be put back into society by recycling it. If a carrot is eaten and some is left behind then the leftover carrot can be made into a meal, or put in a caddy bin for recycling and eventually used for compost in gardens. Whether you are an eco-friendly enthusiast, a working parent or a single individual, you can make a difference and have an impact on the world around you by doing your bit to recycle. And you never know – the less waste we produce could mean our local taxes go down. That would be a nice result, wouldn't it?

It's strange how I'm so fascinated with waste in general. Food waste is my priority right now, but I would like to expand my knowledge. Learning is something that is continuous and is always being updated. I love to learn different things, and the environment information is more important than I thought. I believe people are seeing things differently now, and this is because of the media.

Not a Wasted Experience – a Valuable Lesson

The earliest experience of food waste that I can remember was being in a Chinese restaurant. It was an all-you-can-eat buffet, and I was very overwhelmed, and hungry. I was with an old friend, and the first time we went up we had a plate stacked with delicious food: noodles, rice, spring rolls and fried vegetables. I finished my plate and went up for more, wanting to eat as much as I could. I got to the second bite on another spring roll and began to feel very full. There was still quite a bit of food on the plate, but we decided to leave because we were both full. I remember a young Chinese girl picking my plate up, seeing the food left over and giving me a strange look. At first I was taken aback. What had I done? I had paid my money and left peacefully so I was a little puzzled.

At the time I thought, "All they have to do is scrape it away. What's the problem?" It's funny because it took a long time for me to realise why she wasn't happy with me. It was only after three years that I realised in some parts of Asia it is considered impolite to not finish your food.

Another early experience was doing volunteer work at a farm in Devon. To see the work that goes into an organic vegetable farm just to provide food for people to eat is incredible. Land doesn't mean too much to city folks these days because we are so far removed from our food: dirt removed from potatoes; chickens without feathers, legs or a head; red meat cut and prepared.

It's funny how food is made by machines now, and we use machines to pay for food, and we use machines to take food away. I think doing things manually is the way forward, taking responsibility for what we do.

Food Waste in the UK

Food waste is an environmental, economical and a social concern. The media have really taken a great interest in food waste, and people's awareness has heightened too. The largest producer of food waste in the United Kingdom is the domestic household. Combating food waste was one of the initial goals of the Women's Institutes (WI, a British community-based organisation for women). For World War II, rationing came into effect immediately. Legislation was passed that meant people could be imprisoned for wasting food, and there were posters to encourage people to use kitchen waste to feed animals – primarily swine, but also poultry.

Many of the methods suggested by current campaigns to prevent food waste take inspiration from World War II. In 2000, the government created the Waste & Resources Action Programme (WRAP), a government-funded non-profit company that advises on how to reduce waste and use resources efficiently. In 2007, WRAP launched the "Love Food, Hate Waste" campaign and put food waste issues on the map in the UK.

I'm very proud to work in the food waste sector, plus I enjoy what I do. Food waste images always look dull, but now I plan on making it more vibrant and exciting; adding some spice and making things more interesting. I have already helped food waste gain popularity throughout the south-west, so now I plan to do it in more areas and see how far I can take it. I never thought this would interest me. If someone had said to me when I was at school, "Shane, you will have a passion for cooking with food that people are going to throw away" I would have laughed in their face. It's just fun to do this; a tasty hobby, you could say. What's great is that food websites are being created all the time, and hopefully other chefs will start to create meals from food that they would waste, and things will head in a different direction.

Environmental Issues in the UK

The biggest environmental issues in the UK are: **air pollution**, **climate**

change, **litter** and **waste**. I remember being in a meeting with other environmentalists, and looking around feeling really good that these individuals and organizations felt so passionately and were coming together to do something. People can do so much collectively. Sometimes people can come across as too forward in their pursuit of their goals. The key thing is to make something serious into something positive and fun. If I was stone-faced, ordering people not to waste and forcing leaflets into their hands, would I be successful? I doubt it, because they would feel pushed into a corner.

Main wasted products include:

Bread	Instead of keeping some bread out and freezing the rest, people keep all the bread out, but it ends up not being eaten in time and goes mouldy.
Potatoes	People see that a potato has sprouted and decide to throw it away instead of trimming it and using it.
Salad	Salad is disposed of in the greatest proportion because it is bought regularly and not consumed in three days. Within this time it becomes limp and wet and unattractive.

The 8 Forms of Food Waste

The food industry produces large amounts of food waste too, with supermarkets wasting items which are damaged or unsold but often still edible. This is called 'surplus food'. Food waste puts a large burden on the finances of each household and local council in the UK. Households pay for the collection and disposal of food waste by their local council in the form of council tax. For councils, the cost of food waste comes from its collection and disposal as a part of the waste stream.

Food waste comes in eight forms. This is helpful to think about the next time you look at food. These forms are:

Left on plate	You would eat it but you'll be too full up – This can be kept in fridge or freeze it (depending on what it is).
Leftovers	Leftover skins or other edible/inedible leftovers.

Looks bad	Our eyes tell us that it's horrible but, it could be fine to eat.
Out of date	There's a fine line, you have to really check it out (smell or taste) before you eat it.
Inedible	I can't eat it or I'll be sick.
Smelt bad	Throw it away.
Kept too long	Throw it away.
Mouldy	No way should you eat it.

Lets Go Shopping

To reduce the food waste produced by consumers, campaigns and articles have put forward varying advice and suggestions. Try the following strategies:

Check	Understanding food date labels is very helpful when shopping.
Plan	Before food shopping – using a shopping list or having a really good memory.
Use leftovers	This is the best and most effective way to avoid waste, plus you get to eat more food – hopefully healthy food.

Buy one, get one free (BOGOF) offers have been criticised for encouraging customers to purchase food items that are eventually thrown away. We often buy things we don't need, based on a tempting sale. Understanding food storage and food date labels is very important. Food dates are not understood by consumers; people interpret a best before date as a use by date. Leftover foods can be and are encouraged to be used in other meals, but this isn't done based on "lack of confidence". This is where I come in, hopefully giving people a better insight into how to create meals from wasted food.

Plastic Bags vs. Cotton Bags

Shopping – what a task it is. Have you ever had a plastic bag break on you when you forgot to double bag it? It's the worst thing ever; nightmare. But there is another option: material bags instead. Durable, cute-looking, and they fold up and go in your handbag or pocket. The only drawback is: what if you forget it? You either pay for another one or get a free plastic bag. I have some plastic bag information:

500 billion	The number of plastic carrier bags used worldwide each year.
Ten billion	The number of plastic bags given out in 2008 in the UK. Enough to fill nearly 200 Olympic-sized swimming pools. This roughly equates to 400 per household (Source: DEFRA).
Thousands	Thousands of marine animals and more than one million birds die each year as a result of plastic pollution.
Plastic bags	They not only litter the landscape, but in flood conditions they block drains and pipes, contributing to critical conditions.

So, What Are the Retailers Doing?

Most of them now ask if you need a bag; some are setting up collection points to encourage recycling; and more and more have started to charge for plastic bags to try and stop us from using them. As individuals, we can all help to reduce the number of plastic bags being used by using longer lasting reusable shopping bags. All you need to do is remember to take these with you when you go shopping, and already you'll be helping and doing your part for the environment – plus you can carry more shopping with you.

Waste Management Concepts

Food waste has management concepts to keep things in order. The waste hierarchy which is: prevention, minimisation, reuse, recycling, energy and disposal, remains the cornerstone of most waste minimisation strategies. It refers to the '3 Rs' – **reduce**, **reuse** and **recycle** – which classify waste management strategies according to their desirability in terms of waste minimisation. The aim of the waste hierarchy is to extract the maximum practical benefits from products and to generate the minimum amount of waste. If you look up Waste Management Concept on the Internet, you will see how useful it is to keep this in mind.

Food Waste Organisations

FareShare is a national UK charity supporting communities to relieve food poverty. FareShare is at the centre of two of the most urgent issues that face the UK: food poverty and food waste. It provides quality food to organisations working with disadvantaged people in the community, training and education around the essential life skills of safe food preparation and nutrition, and warehouse employability training through its Skills Training programme, promoting the message that 'No Good Food Should Be Wasted'.

FareShare has been operating since 2004 as an independent charity and today has seventeen locations around the UK. Established in 1994 as a project within the homelessness charity Crisis, FareShare aims to help vulnerable groups, whether they are homeless, elderly, children, or other groups within our communities.

I've had the opportunity to visit FareShare's Bristol headquarters and see the hard work they put in. Knowing what people do behind the scenes really gives me an appreciation for organisation. I've spoken to many workers and they have been very helpful, polite and enthusiastic towards their work.

Foodbank is a non-profit charitable organization that distributes food to those who have difficulty purchasing enough to avoid hunger. It's sad that we've reached this point, but it's amazing that this is a necessary life line for many people in the UK falling on hard times.

WRAP campaign Love Food, Hate Waste aims to raise awareness of the need to reduce food waste and help us all take action. It shows that by doing some easy practical everyday things in the home we can all waste less food, which will ultimately benefit our purses and the environment too. Love Food, Hate Waste is a not-for-profit company. WRAP works in England, Scotland, Wales, and Northern Ireland to help businesses and individuals reap the benefits of reducing waste, develop sustainable products and use resources in an efficient way. I have had the privilege to work alongside them and campaign their message of reducing food waste. I even had the opportunity to feature my recipes on their website, which was a great opportunity for me. Their website is very informative and their members of staff have always been very polite.

Kerry McCarthy, a vegan MP in Bristol, is a patron of FoodCycle and is working to ensure that the pressing issues of food poverty and food waste are on the political agenda, having introduced a Food Waste Bill in 2012.

I first met Kerry at my Veggie Awareness Day in St George. She came along and showed her support for my event, and I approached her in a head to toe cow costume and was surprised she didn't know who I was. After I took if off I introduced myself, spoke for a while and took a picture with her. Its funny looking back at that picture, I had a lot of guts running around St George High Street in a big cow costume giving out vegetarian recipe books. Every time Kerry sees me she says to someone, "I met Shane in a cow suit."

How I See Food

Food, and people's relationship with food in general, is strange. I've used food as a comfort thing, enjoying it for the taste, eating for the occasions, whether I was hungry or not. We buy food in supermarkets and feel as if food is forever growing and infinite. Local food stalls aren't getting the attention because of the convenience of supermarkets. Computers have become the replacement for people. We have self-service because we are on the go, and lining up or having a conversation with someone has become a thing that people don't like to do.

I enjoy talking to people from different generations and other cultures. Everyone has their own way, and everyone thinks that their way is the right way. The more I look into food culture, the more I see how important other countries are for the import of vegetables, fruit, herbs and spices.

By cooking more and becoming a vegetarian, I have become more in touch with food. Before becoming a vegetarian, I had no need to look at the back of food packaging; I forgot there was an ingredients list. When I did start looking and questioning what was in my food my view changed and I started to wonder why these unpronounceable ingredients were there. Also, cooking helped me to appreciate the time and work that goes into making something. Factories are the chefs for most people: they make our bread and everything else. Until you go to an actual bakery (and not commercial bakeries that bake frozen bread but the real bakers) you will never discover what real bread tastes like.

The most annoying thing about food is the snacks. You know they are devoid of nutrients and aren't that great for you, but they taste so nice. I'm glad wholefood store crisps are popping up in commercial supermarkets, containing less oil and more natural ingredients. Until you compare things, you never really know what the differences are. If you have two cookies and one has six ingredients and the other fifteen then you can assess why there are more ingredients in one and whether they will be beneficial.

Sometimes people don't care what food has in it. I've been there – where I was just too hungry to care. But any food you eat has an effect on your body, so it's best to be aware of what may happen if you eat this kind of food regularly. The old saying "you are what you eat" really does hold true. I urge you to educate yourself, find out as much as you can about nutrition, and ensure that the food you eat is the best you can afford.

Am I a Cook?

I prepare food, which would make me a 'preparer' (if that's a word), and I cook which makes me a 'cook'. I use the word 'chef' because I create food for a living. I don't see myself as the best or the worst, just someone that can make nice food. I look through recipe books and select meals that I'd like to try. Once I've mastered the basics, I put a twist on it and make it my own. Creativity is always to be encouraged in the kitchen. The last thing I want to be is generic. When I make something, I give it an interesting name.

My mum would make the most random things, but they tasted good. With a combination of raw ingredients from the cupboard, and some imagination, you can have some very tasty food. Recipes are only guides, a template which can be edited and expanded upon.

I would say any meal that you can make well can be made into a variation. For example, beans on toast. Easy, right? Baked beans heated, toasted bread and that's it. Now look at the variations:

Meal 1	Baked beans, toasted bread, butter and cheese.
Meal 2	Baked beans, black pepper, butter, Worcestershire sauce and cheese.
Meal 3	Baked beans, chives, ketchup, butter, Worcestershire sauce and cheese.

The list can go on, but this is just an example of taking one guide to a meal and expanding on it to your taste and preference.

First Memories of Cooking

My first memory of food was wrapped up in smell – lots of different smells and aromas. I lived in a multicultural environment so I would smell foods from different countries. They would be fish and chips, pies and pasties, curries, noodles, sweet and sour, and patties. I would go to my friends' houses and watch their mothers cook food. Many Asian and Caribbean women don't use weighing equipment but just judge it by doing it repetitively. How does a pianist know how to play a piece by memory? How does a gymnast know how to land when doing a flip? They just know; it's a feeling or hunch. The same goes for cooking: you judge things.

My mum was (and still is) a very good cook. When I was young, she made everything from scratch, and I would watch in the kitchen. I would ask lots of questions because I was curious, and because I was hungry and wanted her to hurry up and feed me. We had a huge cooking book, and I would just select something for her to make, and she would make it. The book had the most beautiful pictures of cakes; I couldn't believe that dry ingredients could be turned into something so tasty. I love food that looks attractive, like you could just eat the pages or smell the aroma from the photos. My sister and I would make jam tarts with leftover pastry, and little rice krispie cakes, and lick the bowls that had the cake mixture in them. We liked to have competitions to see who made the best ones, but my mum always said we both won, which we didn't like to hear. I enjoyed cooking and presentation. I liked things to look neat.

It's funny now because my mum and my sister are pescatarians (they don't eat meat but do eat fish) because of the leaflets and information I would give when we all lived in the same house. My sister likes to remind me that she was a vegetarian first, so she does bring that up when I get cheeky. When she told me she was a vegetarian, at that time I was very unsupportive. I didn't see why she wouldn't eat meat; it's natural, tastes nice, and everyone else eats it. It just seemed abnormal and a little out there to 'only eat vegetables'. So it's funny that now I am a vegetarian as well; very ironic.

At school I enjoyed cooking, but I never saw it as a skill because it came so easily. I would make pancakes, cookies and pizzas. I think it's a great confidence boost to make easy things first and progress. I loved to take these simple things home and show off what I'd made. Cooking is an underrated talent.

School meals were nice when I was young. In nursery, we would have snacks like apples, cheese and milk. And for dinner it would be rice and something else. In junior school, anything with chips was great, plus lasagna and shepherd's pie. When I got to primary and secondary school, eating out was better than eating in, unless they had chips, pizza, burgers or wraps. The things I would eat were chicken, cheese and onion pasties, battered sausage and chips, burger and chips, sweet and sour balls with chips, and lots of snacks for lunch. It was cool to have those things, plus they were food on the go and we didn't have to sit down to eat them. The sit-down food, we would call it, was only eaten by the teachers. They liked the 'proper food' that needed cutlery. Also, we never drank the water at school; it was so warm. I remember seeing Jamie Oliver on his journey to improve school food and thinking, I wonder what he ate as a child? If I eat chips and pizza as an adolescent, and then grow up and discover it's not that great and stop another young person from tasting the same pleasures as me, am I in the wrong or in the right? It's something I've thought about: trying to meet people as close to the middle as possible. For example, if someone wants chips and pizza, and the school wants something more nutritious, then I give them that but in a pizza and chips form. Have the base of the pizza made from wholewheat flour instead of white flour, and more fresh toppings accompanied by salad. And as for the chips, either use chunky chips made from chopped potatoes, wedges with the skin on, or use an oven and not a deep-fat fryer. I'm always trying to bend the rules a little and do something that can please both parties.

Watchers Like to Watch, Chefs Like to Cook

The problem with watching chefs cook is that many people do just that: they 'watch'. We admire what they cook, but are reluctant to make it ourselves. Watching a meal being prepared takes thirty minutes; to prepare it ourselves takes twenty minutes and lots of pots and pans. Then, when the meal is finished, we have to wash it up, and people just don't have the time or patience.

We are living in an age now where speed is the master. We want things more quickly, and at our disposal now. We can have instant everything now, so we don't really have to do much. There are pros and cons to this, but the key thing is being conscious of it. If I ever had a TV show then I would do things differently. I am a very analytical person. You look at a TV show, and look closely and see everything in the frame. The kitchens look like they've come out of a showroom: every pot and pan in existence hanging down, all the different knives, lights making the kitchen look amazing, and the happy-go-lucky chef showing how to cook a meal. I wish the kitchens looked more like everyday kitchens; I wish they used fewer pans and less fancy equipment. Also, do you notice how they never use the fridge?

All the food they use happens to be already out in clear bowls. Is that realistic?

Too Many Cooks…

I've had the unfortunate experience of working with chefs who have very big egos. They take themselves and what they do too seriously in my opinion. What's funny is that eighty per cent of photos/pictures of chefs show them either not smiling or with their arms crossed over their chest. It's such a defensive position, but why? I've been around so many great cooks who really include everyone in the process of cooking, and act as a great example of being a jolly chef that people respect. These guys and girls are who I take inspiration from to develop my personality.

I remember I wanted to do something for Christmas, so I volunteered as an assistant chef at the Julian House's Caring at Christmas. I was a volunteer assistant chef to a lead chef, and we were cooking for over 500 men and women on Christmas Eve and Christmas Day. It was overwhelming being in a kitchen with so many volunteers, and having the responsibility of cooking for people who really needed this meal. I chopped vegetables and collaborated with the chef in charge. At the end of the shift, it felt good to have prepared a meal that lots of people were going to enjoy. The next year, I said I would go for the head chef position and lead volunteers. We had to discuss the menu, and go through health and safety and how the kitchen worked. I'm not going to lie: I was very nervous. I was thinking, OK, now I'm in the deep end. If I mess up, people won't eat, and I'll be responsible.

The kitchen was huge. I've never been in such a big kitchen. Everything was there; the store cupboard was huge too. I've never seen so many raw ingredients. Shelves full of mince pies, soups, vegetables and fruits. All this food I could use, all of it. I was in food dreamland.

How was I going to deal with four teams of volunteers for two days? I came in, signed in and was briefed about the ethos of doing this work. I put my things away in the locker, put my chef whites on, and waited in the kitchen downstairs for the volunteers. It's so funny now because it seems like such a long time ago that this happened.

I was in the kitchen and I started to hear everyone come in. I was the chef, and everyone was lined up (fifteen volunteers, I think) and looking at me for directions. Everyone was looking at me and they were silent, so I was thinking, wow, I'm like the captain right now. I explained who I was and what we were going to do. I asked them to wash their hands and assigned everyone to a desired role. Leading a team is not an easy process. It's not assigning the role that's difficult, but making sure everyone is happy in their role. The atmosphere is the key to anything. The volunteers were great, but I had to keep spirits high and make sure people had a taste of doing different roles.

Vegetables were being chopped, cakes were being made, and everyone was happy. Now, the turkey I knew I would be cooking, so I had to read some recipe books on how to prepare it as it had been so long since I'd done one. It felt strange looking at the turkey, but I did prepare it. I have to say I didn't have the guts to actually slice it, so I assigned someone else to do that for me. Once everything was cooked, we put it in the hot trays and waited until everyone was lined up. It was amazing: all these volunteers who didn't know each other coming together for the two most important days in a Western year (Christmas Eve and Christmas Day). It was a great thing, and serving the food was amazing. The presentation was incredible and the smell was amazing. The guests (homeless men and women) were very humble and appreciated the food. We were eating mince pies and having a great time in the kitchen too. Once the shift was over, I said goodbye to the volunteers and changed with another chef. The shift was over; the food had been cooked; everyone was happy. Then I remembered, wow, now I have to do the same thing tomorrow with another group of volunteers. I was more confident the second time because I really knew what to expect. After those two days were over, I felt great. I look back and smile. That was an exceptional experience. I always say that volunteering was where I got my real training. That experience was as valuable as any course or book.

Angry Chefs

Have you seen them? To prove my theory right about angry chefs, write 'chef' in a search engine and see what images you get. Whether they are smiling or not, notice their arms. The crossed defensive arms are very noticeable. In addition, these chefs tend to dominate people. Take Gordon Ramsay for example, whether he is actually like that in real life or not, I don't like that image. That's what makes people not want to cook, or get into the profession. Why are they so angry and grumpy? If you don't like your profession then don't be in it.

Don't let the chef's whites intimidate you. Cooking shouldn't be intimidating. Remember, cooking food existed before restaurants and white coats. We all ate with our hands at one time, so don't let using a knife and fork or etiquette at the table throw you off.

I like the happy depictions of chefs from when I was young. Remember *Lady and the Tramp*? There was a chef called Joe. White hat, moustache, smiley and a little eccentric. Stereotypyical, but it was a nice look. Also the vintage jolly baker with the big white hat, big stomach and a big smile on his face. You don't have to have a Father Christmas stomach, but I like the jolly baker look so maybe, subconsciously, I incorporated that into myself without knowing. There are some people who wear the modern hats, or their hat is black. I'm not a fan of any modern chef stuff; I like the traditional Italian style instead.

Spiritual Cooking

What does spiritual cooking mean? Cooking for the gods, or that the gods cook and I take credit for it? No, it means a deep understanding that what you cook affects a person deeper then we can ever know. There's something very spiritual about cooking. Someone is creating a meal with their hands, all for you to consume with your mouth. I believe angry chefs bring bad vibes to their cooking, and their establishment. So many things happen behind the scenes when you work with a team, and if there are bad vibes I believe you can feel it when you have your plate of food.

Ever had a happy chip shop owner, chef, sandwich guy or anyone else cook for you and present you food with a happy face? How did you feel when you ate it? And have you had a meal given to you by an angry cook? How did you feel? I've experienced both. It's like the happy cook makes the food taste better by their smile, and the angry cook kind of dampens the experience of the meal.

From these experiences, I make sure that I am happy whatever I'm doing. People see this and it is like a magnet. I would like to think that I'm a happy cook/chef, and my cooking is spiritual; I am aware of my ingredients and I am making it with care and positive thoughts. I remember going into a restaurant/cafeteria. Before I even had a chance to look at the menu, the chef said, "CAN I HELP YOU?" in a really sharp way, with a harsh voice. I said I was looking at the menu, and he looked very upset; like moody mixed with grumpy, and that's some bad maths. So, I told him what I wanted. He made the food, and handed it to me and looked really annoyed. I ate the food, but I didn't want to because of that negative energy going into the food.

Chefs on TV

I feel the way chefs are portrayed on TV is a problem. What are some of them actually teaching us? The editing team must have a field day giving us all the juicy arguments and tantrums, even though they are entertaining. When we think 'chef', what comes in our mind? Now, it's about dominance, competition, being in charge and panicking. Tears and sweat, shouting, et cetera; it's just the wrong type of message. How did it get like this? I like collaboration, not dominance. I don't mind people knowing their role as a chef, but I don't like it when one overpowers the other and people feel dominated. I hope we can get to a point where chefs make easy recipes, something quick, show what they do with wasted food (with compostable bags and caddies in view), and stay away from scales and start using measuring spoons. This would revolutionise things for the better. It only takes one chef to start this, and hopefully this subject on food waste and cooking on a budget thing will catch on. Not everyone has the time and finances to shop in lavish wholefood stores, or cook difficult meals from scratch every day. There are a lot of chefs now who are doing their part, but I hope more will follow.

What Chefs Do I Like, Then?

There aren't many chefs that I really respect, which is a shame. Anyone who is a famous chef obviously has skills in cooking, but it's more about their attitude than anything else.

We're in an age where names matter, and it seems like you need a name to be called chef. There are many chefs in many restaurants and cafés, but because of their dedication to their craft, they are unable to take a risk and really do things differently. I am more of a freelance experimental chef, never based anywhere but I'm everywhere.

There are only two chefs that I really like:

Jamie Oliver – I have respect for Jamie, and his journey from being an unknown chef to a respected recognised figure in cooking and education. *Jamie's School Dinners* was what really made me notice what he was doing. The fact that he was so passionate about his work, and was willing to dedicate so much of his time to it really impressed me. Also, he was trying to change government policy and people's views on food too. We have a similar passion, but we are doing different things.

Hugh Fearnley-Whittingstall – I like River Cottage, plus his rustic approach to cooking. I really enjoyed his vegetarian special. I wish others would do the same.

Notable Homages

These are people I respect for being black British chefs on TV:

Ainsley Harriott – I liked *Can't Cook, Won't Cook,* and *Ready Steady Cook.* I liked his personality and that he made food comical and entertaining.

Lorraine Pascale – I love the food she makes, it looks really tasty. I saw her on TV and enjoyed her personality and the programme.

Levi Roots – It was great seeing someone from *Dragon's Den* doing something successful with his cooking and his sauce. I had the opportunity to meet him in Cheltenham. He was very polite and humble.

Rustie Lee – She was the first chef I ever saw on TV. I have to say I was a little shocked by her cooking technique at that time because she used the blood and everything from the animals she was cooking. Now I see that as a good thing. My vegetarian side turns a blind eye, as at least she is using everything and not wasting parts of the animal.

I think that showing homage and respect towards people is very important, especially the dead. I believe people die when you stop talking about them and keep their name below water.

There were a lot of important vegetarians in history, but the following are the two who are local (UK based) and deserve the homage. This isn't a lengthy biography on them, but if this quick overview interests you then you can research the names further.

Donald Watson – Who? Who's this guy? It's not surprising that the general public doesn't know who he is, but you would think the vegan community would. Most of the vegans I know don't know who he is.

Donald Watson was founder of the Vegan Society and inventor of the word vegan. His vision: he didn't want to harm any living thing but still wanted to live a happy life and enjoy food in the process. I never knew who he was, because no one spoke about him or the origin of the word vegan before. I respect any pioneer or someone who sparks a movement. Many friends I know say, "I don't want to hurt animals. I just like how they taste." I can definitely identify with them because I felt that way at one time. It's incredible that Donald lived till he was ninety-five years old. I would love to live to that age. Imagine the wisdom you can acquire by seeing so much. When I first heard about him, I searched for him on a search engine to see what he looked like. He seemed like a cool guy, very relaxed. The fact that he was an active man is a great example to anyone at any age to keep busy and live their life.

Kathleen Jannaway – It's funny because I had never heard of this lady until I stumbled across some information about her. I was at a vegan event when I made a donation to a lady who was selling a Compassionate Living booklet. It was a small booklet containing some recipes and also stories about people. I read the story of Kathleen Jannaway. It was a sweet story and very thought-provoking. Kathleen Jannaway was born in 1915 in London. Her mother died shortly after Kathleen's birth. Her father had been disabled by TB in his hip as a boy and only outlived his wife by a few years. Kathleen was an only child and was brought up by her paternal grandparents. She described her childhood as hard and impoverished. Her grandmother was a good manager and never allowed them to go hungry.

Kathleen was a bright child and won a scholarship to the County Secondary School. After successfully passing her school certificate she then trained as a junior school teacher at a Training College. She taught in several London schools as a biology teacher.

In 1938 Kathleen married her husband, Jack. They spent the first part of the war living in Sussex where they became vegetarians. Kathleen recalled that, as she watched lambs in the fields and was slicing up their roast lamb, they both decided at precisely the same time not to eat meat again.

Kathleen taught in the local school. She and Jack moved into a cottage on the farm where Jack worked and Kathleen cycled along the railway line to work. They had a son called Richard who was born in 1945. A bomb destroyed their cottage and this had a profound and upsetting effect on Kathleen.

After the war, Kathleen had two children named Mary and Patrick. Kathleen devoted the next fifteen years of her life to her family. She taught children with learning difficulties and transferred to a special centre doing pioneering work with children with dyslexia and developing new teaching materials. At the same time the whole family attended a Dorking Quaker meeting and became members. Kathleen was soon very involved with the children's committee and the work of the Quakers. Actively campaigning for peace, she and Jack were founder members of Quaker Green Concern, now Quaker Green Action. Kathleen was an active member of a group in Leatherhead during the Freedom from Hunger Campaign.

Jack's death in 1999 was an enormous blow. Kathleen insisted, however, on moving to a new home in Devon. This was shared with her daughter and son, and she briefly enjoyed the beauty and the challenge of the new garden. Kathleen remained active, researching and writing. Her amazing thirst for knowledge was unquenchable: she was an avid reader until her eyesight began to fail significantly in the last year of her life. Kathleen continued to campaign for tree planting to combat global warming, and to spread the other MCL messages (Movement for Compassionate Living) until illness and exhaustion overcame her and she died in 2003.

To come from humble beginnings, hardwork to gain an education and work with children with learning difficulties was a commendable thing to do. I like her philosophy of compassion and practising what you preach. The photos of Kathleen are very endearing and add to the story; old black and white pictures from the past always add a sentimental vintage look at a different era. Even if she hadn't been a vegetarian (which she was, vegetarian and then vegan) it is still a story about dedication, triumph and strength.

Thinking about it now, that's what I want this book to be: about food, but more about thought. It's great to be able to be transparent and open my life to other people, even in a couple of words. It can be scary too, but I've always been a guy who's prepared to take educated risks. The story of Kathleen Jannaway never preached, but allowed the reader to see for themselves what it was trying to portray. I hope I will be able to do the same.

Food As a Weapon

A weapon can hurt people, and food definitely can be used as a weapon. I really dislike it when someone intimidates people with lavish words that mean simple things. Anything, whether it's art, music or literature, can be used in an elitist way. Some cook for fun, to experiment and share, and don't take things too seriously. Others see food as an art that has to be done a certain way: meaning the right cutlery, the correct way of eating, watching your posture, speech, and the correct wine to drink. If you don't follow these rules then you're frowned upon. Wow, all this for food.

Some people say to me, "Would you like to own your own restaurant one day?" I don't think I would have a restaurant, but perhaps a café that people can come to for a pleasant meal. A place that looks smart with open windows, but not a showy place where you have to dress too over the top. Maybe the odd night but not to the extent of it being labelled 'posh'.

Pretentious Foods and Their Real Names:

Pretentious – what does it mean? Attempting to impress by affecting greater importance, talent, culture, et cetera, than is actually possessed. Basically, showy food. For example, today I went to a restaurant and had a plate of warm ciabatta bread, topped with creamy feta cheese and smoked prosciutto ham. OK, so you basically had hot bread, cheese and ham, but that doesn't sound as fancy now, does it?

Prosciutto	Ham
Fois gras	Liver
Potato rosti	Fried potatoes
Empanada	Pasty
Gazpacho	Cold soup
Cioppino	Fish soup

I always say anything French, Italian or Spanish sounds better on a menu; the English language doesn't seem to have the same effect. It would be good to see old classic British cuisine on menus more, because the food (regardless of it being meat) is mixed in the tradition, and even some medieval dishes would look great on a modern-day plate.

Bristol, More Than Just a Bridge

Bristol is in the south-west of England. Instead of giving you a standard account of Bristol, I'll tell you what it's like from my perspective. Bristol is a very interesting place to live. It has a great mix of food and culture that makes the city unique. I never realised how diverse it was until I moved away. There are food stalls, markets, street food, whole food stores and so much more. It has a place for everyone, and you can get many things from different areas. Most Asian shops stock Caribbean ingredients. Corner shops sell Polish foods. The diversity is exciting. What I like most is that there are the usual stereotypical 'posh' restaurants that require ties and suits to get into, and there are also cafés just run by volunteers that welcome everyone. Every area has its own flavor, its own personality and brings its own style. When I think of Bristol, I don't think of Brunel's bridge or Clifton Village, but high-rise buildings and people. Regardless of how you see Bristol, food runs that city. There are many events and celebrations: Easton has its Community Centre that has great food, including FoodCycle and other meals and events. Stokes Croft and Gloucester Road have a great mix of food and culture, and St Paul's has a lot of Caribbean and West Indian food.

Everywhere has its social problems, and Bristol is not excluded from this, but I'll definitely say it's like a little London. The key to knowing Bristol is to explore as many areas as possible: not just the city centre and tourist areas, but the hidden areas too. Each spot has its own little style, and it's great to see that. I've been to most of the areas in Bristol, and that has given me a deeper and wider perspective on people, social issues and food.

The best way to see Bristol is to meet a Bristolian (even though I don't call myself that) and allow them to show you around. It is a big city and doing this alone can be overwhelming. Things to check out are Bristol Food Connections Festival (one of the best food festivals in the UK); Vegfest (UK's biggest festival of vegetarian food and environmental information); The Harbourside Festival; Big Green Week; and Feeding the 5000.

I think the great thing about any place (city, town or village) is to check out as many areas as possible. If your area doesn't have a wide range of food then ask for it; if you can't get it, make it. It doesn't have to be food and spices from other cultures, but local food too. Food is the culmination of history, hard work and dedication from farmers.

Even though I was brought up with a lot of Caribbean and Asian food, I loved British cuisine, and still do. For example: full English breakfast, fish and chips, Sunday roast, shepherd's pie, bangers and mash with beans, Cornish pasties and Yorkshire puddings. It may seem strange a vegetarian telling you this, but I never say that meat is bad or wrong. I just decided later on in my life not to eat meat. There are many vegetarians and vegans who have never eaten a piece of meat or a dairy product in their life. I have, but I chose to eat plant-based food without meat or with a meat replacement. I have found that people respect me more because I'm coming from a place of experience and not just guessing.

A Little Place Called Bath

Bath is a small regency city in Somerset, very close to Bristol. It's another place where I've worked a lot. I enjoy Bath very much. Visually, it's one of the prettiest places I've seen. It's like a bigger version of Clifton: that same beautiful Roman sandstone walls, lots of trees and elegance in every corner. I wanted to do some work in Bath so I helped with a group called Green Vision an environmental group that does work in and around Bath. I didn't cook for their organization – they had a head cook – but I did assist and I did a lot of street work: dressing up and giving out leaflets and handing out food. This was great because it gave me a chance to practise my people skills.

It was great that Bath had a group of young people thinking about environmental projects. When I was young, environmental issues meant nothing to me. It was a joke, people picking up litter and recycling. This got me thinking that I wanted to go to schools, do talks and discuss environmental projects; make it fun, link it to the curriculum and get people (teachers and young people) to start thinking about things from a different angle.

I had a chance to meet the mayor and mayoress of Bath on two occasions, and they were very nice and sociable. I liked the support they showed for food and environmental projects. It was very inspiring. Also

I loved Green Park Station where there was a market: local people making food and selling fruit and vegetables is really great. It gave me a look at the past where farmers' markets and stalls were common; no superstores. Don't get me wrong – superstores have their advantages, but it's nice to have a balance.

In addition to this, I went to Transition Bath meetings. It was great to meet so many driven people that want to do something to help climate change and local environmental issues. Everyone has their own skills and they are willing to do what they can to help. Meeting similar like-minded people is so positive when you are doing solo projects. You are able to network and find out what other people are doing. You can either join their project, they can join yours, or you can create a new one. Also these experiences have led to my ideas, creativity and success.

Bristol and Bath are definitely two places that have shaped my mindset, and the places I will do the most work when it comes to food, education and environmental issues.

What is Kabele?

Kabele is a very unique building because it does so much. It's a community centre, café, bike workshop, conference meeting area and so much more. Café Kabele was a strange experience at first. It has a strange name (which I couldn't pronounce) and was hard to find. I remember meeting a friend and trying to find vegetarian and vegan places to eat. We arranged to meet up and check out Kabele, and, when we went in, it was a little awkward. We went there on a protest meeting night. Everyone was wearing lots of black and had tattoos, and there were lots of signs around that were unfamiliar. At first I was like, hmm...maybe I need to leave. But, after seeing the delicious food, I decided to stay. The material was a little controversial, borderline ideology, but if I read between the lines I could learn a lot.

It was a great place for me to experiment. I would cook breakfast for campaigners and help with evening meals. For inspiration, I would look things up on the Internet to make and then replicate them and put my own twist on them. People enjoyed my food, and that's how I got my confidence to start experimenting. I felt like a food scientist; it felt good. Plus it gave me a chance to try out herbs and spices in combination, to know how the kitchen works and how stock is assessed and daily duties like that. I haven't spoken to ninety per cent of the people the cooking evenings since then, but I still respect them. At the time, the community feel was great. It was a great place to hang out in amongst like-minded people, eating, drinking (no alcohol), and enjoying the space and the environment. I've noticed, and this is just a personal opinion, that vegetarians (Lacto-ovo-vegetarians) seem to be more easy-going than vegans. I've been around both for years, and there is definitely a difference. Even though the vegans I knew were cool, there was a great emphasis on dissecting their beliefs. Vegan, animal rights and anarchist views seem to be either intertwined or separate. You could be a vegan, but someone might have a problem with you being with a certain bank, or a university that does medical experiments or funds the arms trade. This was where I felt that I was in a different place to everyone else. It became too serious for me, and I wanted to take a more light-hearted approach. I see it like this: everyone has problems, and we try our best to do something that can alleviate problems and to enjoy things. Being angry about animals being used for meat, angry about the dairy farms, angry about the banks supposedly funding the war, and keeping within a clique is not for me.

In my opinion, after meeting vegans all over the UK, I would set these as loose categories of vegans:

Dietary vegan	This is someone who eats vegan but doesn't wear vegan – might wear leather, wool, etc.
Ethical vegan	Someone who wears vegan but doesn't eat vegan.
Commercial	A commercial vegan is someone who eats commercial vegan food – processed vegan burgers, crisps, chocolates, etc.
Home-cook	A home-cook vegan is someone who eats only cooked food using fresh ingredients, no processed meals, etc.

The Arc Cafe

The Arc Café is in Broadmead, Bristol. I started working there for a while and developed new, interesting recipes. FoodCycle gave me a base to experiment, but the Arc Café gave me an opportunity to try my first food waste experiment: banana skin curry. I remember having a banana (or two) and putting the skin in the caddy bin. I looked at how much room there was before I put the banana skin in, and thought, I wish banana skin was edible. I said this out loud and a colleague said it was, so I decided to do some independent research.

It allowed me to open my mind to different things, and see things from a worldly view and not just a Western viewpoint. It was a learning experience and triggered different things in my life. My mindset changed as I began research all the work that goes into the food, from the people who grow the food, the lorries that travel through the night to bring the food in the supermarket and the staff that wake up early in the morning to stock the shelves for us to look around. The closest thing I have experienced to being exposed to an empty supermarket is Christmas time when everyone buys in bulk. When I look through British history it was important for survival to catch food such as meat and fish, and to learn how to harvest vegetables. Now we are at the point where we eat fish and have no idea how they are caught or the work fishermen put it; we never see animals being killed for meat or hung up, and a lot of people have never planted vegetables. Food is valuable and a necessity. Food brings us happy memories, colour and culture.

This is where people's fascination, and mine too, started with what could be turned into a meal. The newspapers came and tried my banana skin curry, and people liked it very much, but they just didn't believe there was actually banana skin in it. They would say, "I can't taste it. It doesn't taste like banana!" It's true; it doesn't taste like banana, or anything. It's like a nutritious piece of nothing, like tofu or mushrooms, but it can be spiced with anything to make a nice flavour. I started researching in a deeper way, and looking at what was thrown away and what could be salvaged and made into a meal. I saw this as a financial money-saving thing and from an environmental perspective.

Like anywhere I've worked, I took something from the Arc Café experience. Being in commercial cafés taught me to see what was happening behind the scenes; to look at how to order and track stock, ingredients' prices, and dealing with wholesalers. Volunteering helped me to get formal and informal training, meet new people, and work in a sector that I hadn't worked in. Some people see volunteer work as a strange concept because money isn't exchanged. People don't realise that experience replaces the money; you can't buy experience. No matter how many books you read on a subject or how many times you ask someone something, doing it yourself and gaining that know-how is vital.

There were some professions that I wanted to do, but after getting a taste of them, I decided not to. For example, I like basketball and enjoy it for the thrill of the game, but having to practise every day and actually do plays and drills would bore me as a professional. I wanted to draw portraits when I was younger, but I realised that my passion lay in drawing as a leisure activity rather than as a professional artist going to Art School. Basketball and art were more hobbies than career plans, but I was definitely interested in doing something that I would genuinely enjoy.

My Time at FoodCycle

FoodCycle is a non-profit organization that sets up groups of volunteers to collect surplus produce locally and prepare nutritious meals in unused professional kitchen spaces. These meals are served to those in need in the local community.

The organization has its headquarters in London, England and has operations throughout the United Kingdom. My first encounter with food waste was when I joined FoodCycle Bristol. I guess you could call it a turning point in my life when it comes to food. A friend took me to have lunch, so we travelled to Easton Community Centre where I saw people around my age cooking and preparing food. The food smelt great, and I was looking forward to eating it. As we finished our lunch, I saw that there was a collection box that said 'donations' so I decided to make a donation. I saw a girl preparing food with an apron on that said 'foodcycle'. I had never heard of foodcycle before. What did it mean? Food that rides a bike? I asked her what foodcycle was, and how she had got involved. It sounded so interesting to me, and I wanted to be a part of it.

After doing my online food hygiene certificate and induction, I did my first shift in the early hours of Sunday morning. The volunteers (mostly girls) were very polite and showed me around the kitchen. At the beginning, it was a waiting game; waiting for the cyclists to bring the wasted food from the local shops and supermarkets. When they arrived, I was in shock to see how much food had been wasted. So much bread I could have made a chair from it, lots of fruit, vegetables and 'mystery food': food I looked at and thought, what the hell is that? I had to buy a food encyclopaedia after working at FoodCycle because I wanted more knowledge on different food. With all this food staring back at me, I wondered, What the hell are we going to make? I was so surprised that two hours in we had come up with an incredible meal for the community. It was like a magic trick, a food magic trick. The people who came into the community centre were very polite and humble, and they loved the food too. We were allowed to have some, and the group dynamic was great. I worked for FoodCycle for around six or seven months, and I never experienced any bad vibes from any of the volunteers.

I have to give respect to Bristol University, because most of the managers and volunteers were students doing degrees, Masters and PHDs, and still coming into the community to cook. They never had an elitist-type mentality at all. Hand on heart, I have nothing negative to say about any students or the FoodCycle experience.

The Journey

I'm not sure if this was learning or training, but it definitely was a turning point. I had the opportunity to go to a two-week break in Devon to learn about food security. It was like a little retreat out in the middle of nowhere and very beautiful. For a city boy like me, this was a welcome treat. There was a big path that took us up to a huge sanctuary, but we camped outside in tents. That was my first experience of camping outside, so I was a little worried about insects and the weather. There were about ten of us, and there was lots of information around, but the day was so jam-packed that we never got a chance to read it all. It was basically about knowing ourselves, knowing other people, and what our strengths and weaknesses were.

We had a chance to be on a farm and see the milking process, and how vegetable farms were kept. The work that went into these organic vegetable farms was incredible. Also, there was an apple tree with the juiciest little red apples I'd ever seen. All this added to its beauty.

Now, let me tell you this. The first week was all light-hearted, but the second week was deep. Deep like the ocean deep, not deep end of the swimming pool deep. There were tears, confessions and everything. It did teach me about myself, and I was very inspired by the goals of everyone else. Now back to the deep part. We had to sit around in a circle and tell people about who we were and what we stood for. I see now that this was a confidence booster, and a way to review our plans to other people and ourselves. Also, they filmed our vision of the future for us; a film I still to this day haven't seen. We also took a group picture and sent a letter to ourselves. That was creepy: getting a letter from myself three months later asking if I had completed my goals. Sounds confusing, right?

I think, on an unconscious level, being there helped me see things from a different perspective. Reflection was the key to the whole experience, and I really took something from it. Another thing that happened was delightful, and also sad. There was a group of young people who were part of a health and well-being retreat. I was told that life had become too much to handle for them, so they were given a break from their lives to spend time in the countryside. We were picking apples, helping with the vegetables and growing plants, and we had the opportunity to speak to them. We didn't mention anything about their problems, just had a friendly talk about what they had been doing there. It was so important to know how being around good food, positive people and some country air could really give them that vitality they needed. I definitely look back with fond memories.

The Backlash

Not everything was as peachy as you may think. When I was doing only vegan things with other vegans, I received positive feedback and encouragement. I could do no wrong, but once I started doing more vegetarian cooking, promoting local food (meat or vegetables) and doing things on a solo basis, I received an unwelcome backlash from my community. I used to be with a group in Bristol, and friends there got me started cooking in food stalls and travelling around the UK. My first public cooking experience came when a particular person (a lady) asked me if I wanted to help at her food stall. She encouraged the cooking side and gave me the outlet to create food and work with the public. At the time, I was unaware that the secret condition was that I was cooking and promoting vegan food. When I switched to vegetarian food her attitude changed and her support left. It didn't loosen or slip away, but was completely withdrawn. When someone helps you start something and (in my opinion) then turns on you when you don't play by their rules, it hurts.

Respect is about value, and when I started to shift and expand my views and way of life I was devalued. I felt disrespected because I realised that friendship wasn't as powerful as politics. Members of the group did not want to be seen by other vegans as supporting someone who was promoting or condoning a vegetarian lifestyle. It was a mixture of others ethics and beliefs against mine, and peer pressure from other vegans in their circle. I had supported all their events and activities but as a friend first, and then as a supporter of the movement.

I saw myself, and still see myself, as being a mainstream person that wants to be the middle man: instead of wanting people to come to me, or wanting to go to them, I'd say "Let's meet in the middle". I hate the 'us versus them' mentality when it comes to food, so I had to make a decision to do things solo or make an alliance with other people. This was a wake-up call because it made me analyse who was around me, what my goals were, and helped make me a stronger person. In any profession we need the courage to stand by what we believe in and never set our minds in stone. I see my mind like water: it can be ice, all hard and set, but, like ice, it can melt and mould and resemble something else; always changing and forming. Negative energy is like smoke: damaging to the body and very toxic. Knowing who's in your circle and who's encouraging you, and who's secretly trying to find faults, is important before you move on to big projects.

After leaving behind the negative people, I found open-minded people with a more naturalistic approach to doing things. They were more concerned with bringing people together than fixed moral views. It was the best thing for me, but I was still sad that this had to happen. The funniest thing was that the same people who didn't support me wanted to congratulate me when I did something successful. Why congratulate something that you don't approve of? That's fake. Why act fake with me? Just say "I don't like what you do" and stand up for your beliefs. The key thing is doing what I believe in and finding others who share the same ethos. I can't please everyone.

Another thing that I became unsure about was whether people were my friends because of what I eat or because of who I am. It made me question things. For example, let's say they saw me out eating a burger. What then? Perhaps they'd say, "That's fine, but what happened to make you do that?" Would I be outcast from the 'clique' or would my actions be frowned upon? Once I started feeling like this, my people had to be assessed, 'my people' referring to vegan people that I socialized with.

I see having lots of people around me as a gift and a curse. Sometimes it's better to have a small circle of people so I know their intentions rather than assuming large numbers of people are thinking the same way. From that point I cut away from big groups and started to do things either in a small group, or independently.

Another important thing is to never assume anything, and always have a back-up plan. I assumed I would have support. I was wrong. I thought things would go to plan. Any event needs a back-up plan, or a personal risk assessment. Never put your faith too much into anything; leave some room just in case. Never assume something will be there, or someone will do something. Carry supplies and have a safety backup plan that aids success. This is logical for me, not a paranoid way of thinking. Success is all about preparation, so be prepared as much as possible. I definitely do that now.

Being Transparent: Everyone Can See Me Now

I realise that people aren't as brave as they say they are. People talk a great game, but when it comes to doing something, they fade away into the background. The people I used to be around stood for something in a group, but never as individuals. I underestimated how much guts a person needs to do anything solo. If I succeed, I'll get all the praise, but if I fail, I get all the criticism and there is no one to fall back on. I like that now, because I'm able to do things my way. What's kind of bitter-sweet is that I had ideas about food waste, recycling, education work and opening information up to the public a long time ago. Unfortunately, people don't like it when someone does things differently. But, when I succeeded with this idea, then everyone wanted to celebrate my success. Now I was creative; now I was amazing. Before that, I was seen as someone who was biting off more than they could chew. It's funny how people change their attitude, isn't it?

Real People, Real Words

The best part about doing anything public is dealing with the public. The public fill me with a mix of amusement and bewilderment, and a touch of mystery. You never know who you're going meet. Some are polite, others curious, some cheeky, and others way out there. The best thing is that people are being real. If you're on a vegetarian stall then they'll say what they think. This is good because you want feedback.

I remember my first time on a food stall, and a guy came up to me and asked me what I had made. I told him a vegan pattie (spicy vegetables in a spicy yellow pastry) and told him to try it. Now, he ate it and said something that always sticks me with. He said, "I don't care if it's vegan or not. If it tastes good then I'll eat it, and this tastes good." No one wants to eat something that's good for them and tastes horrible, but people want to eat things that are not good or nutritious, but taste great. What does that say? Taste is the key to making any point about food. If you make good food and take away the vegetarian labels then you still have good food.

Now, when I was young I had no respect for vegetarians as a whole. I was very vocal about it if I met one (and that was rare). It just didn't make sense to me, because it was never really explained to me. Conversation didn't persuade me in any way. I just made the conscious decision to listen to my body and make adjustments. I later learned that the adjustments I made had a name, and that name was 'vegetarian'. People often talk about not wanting to be 'turned' into a vegetarian or vegan. I laugh sometimes; am I a witch that 'turns' people into something they don't want to be? You can't be turned. And if you can then it's for the wrong reasons. Do what you believe, not what others believe to please them.

Food Stalls

When I was first asked to do a food stall, I declined a million times. It was intimidating to talk to the public, aka people I didn't know, and ask them to try food that I had prepared. It was nerve-racking because it felt like it took them five hours to try a bite of food when it was actually only five seconds. Everyone loves compliments. I guess I just didn't expect so many. Once I'd got a taste of compliments, I wanted more. In addition to food, I had the opportunity to do a stall on recycling. This was great because I was able to hear what people really had to say. I liked being approachable and having an open conversation with people about how they saw recycling in general. I would ask, "Do you recycle your food and plastic bottles?" They would say no, yes, sometimes or I don't really know how to do it. They talked about it as something enforced by the government, but not something they wanted to do for themselves.

This experience was funny in so many ways. For example, if I owned a stall giving away free food, people would see that the sign said vegan and say, "I don't like vegan food." I would laugh to myself. How do they know what it tastes like if they don't eat it? Aren't chips vegan? Beans on toast, humus and falafel in a pitta wrap?

Running stalls also taught me about tone, approach and eye contact. I saw this as a mini-lesson in body language and marketing. I would pretend that I was an actor playing the part of a salesman. First, I would be the loud guy, then the quiet guy, then the sweet guy, and see the reaction. Also, I would ask questions of people who liked the food we gave out, and ask why some people didn't at least want to try some food. I mean, it was free.

Giving people free food is not as easy as you may think. Anything that is free is looked at with scepticism. Why is it free? What's the hidden agenda? I have always said that if we priced everything at £1 and we didn't have a vegetarian sign, then we would have no food left. This got me fascinated about the psychology of how people see food. I decided to take a course in nutrition, and look at the senses and how we like things: what colours, textures, smells et cetera please us.

Also, it made me see things differently. When I go past a food stall, or any stall, I know what it takes to ask a stranger to take a leaflet, try food or even say hello. Some people have the social skills and they are able to do it with ease, and others see it as their ultimate nightmare.

Not Just a One-Trick Pony

I am known for creating unique meals from wasted food, so I am happy with my reputation. But, there was a turning point. I had the opportunity to help at a school in Wales with their eco-friendly week. They asked me what I did, and I told them I specialised in cooking. They said they didn't have the facilities for cooking, and they wondered if I could do anything else. It made me think: am I just a one-trick pony, so to speak? Am I just a cooking guy? I was really annoyed by that, so it made me want to find another lane. I started to get into recycling more, and finding fun activities that I could do with paper and other types of material. I did a workshop with children where we made origami boxes out of old magazines. It was so much fun reusing things that people may have thought was junk or rubbish. The children enjoyed it, I enjoyed it, and so did the teachers. Things like that make me smile because they add new skills to my CV and allow me more scope. I am looking into other things that are environmentally friendly and sustainable now.

School Days and Talks

Talking in front of people can be daunting, but doing talks in schools was interesting. I remember when I had speakers come in to talk about things when I was at school and how interested and fascinated I was with them. It felt strange being the person at the front talking about a subject, and having people looking at me. I thought I would be nervous talking to people, but it was quite relaxing. The fact that I wasn't talking down to the young people, and I brought free snacks with me too, definitely made me popular. By being open with them, they became open with me. The teachers were very open and warm towards my whole approach. They had been a little sceptical because of a previous speaker who had tried to force their ideology of what people should eat. The teachers were not very keen on that approach, and found mine a great contrast.

With younger children, it's great to have prompts: food and things that are visual. In primary schools, secondary schools and community centres, people need more verbal interaction. Visual is great, but allowing people to talk back and voice their opinions is very important.

I wish others would give talks. 'Real life people', whether they're chefs, work on radio, TV or in a shop, can make a point better than a book or a teacher. People are curious about other people's professions.

Events

I remember the first event that I organised myself. I have to say I never knew what work went into an event. I had, and still have, a lot of respect for anyone who manages anything, especially an event to do with food. I decided to do a vegetarian event in a local church on Church Road called Bethesda Church. It would be free food, information, and other treats. Now, I had to take care of so much before the actual event: show my food hygiene certificate and event management certificate; organise the food; the transport of food; volunteers; black bags for clearing away things, et cetera. It was a lot for a couple of hours. That's the thing with events: if you organise something and you do well then you get all the credit, and if you don't do well you get all the blame. Fortunately, I did well with my lovely volunteers, and we had a really successful day. It was in the Evening Post. The MP of St George (Kerry McCarthy) came, and I had the chance to run around in a pig and cow costume in my own area. That was really funny, running around and shaking people's hands, and giving them vegetarian magazines. I wanted it to be playful and fun, and it was. That was a great experience, and the reception was very welcoming. The church didn't mind me using their venue; the money we collected went to an animal charity; and people were talking about the event.

Uncharted Territory

When I do demos, talks and workshops, I try and keep a balance of environments. When you see famous chefs doing these things, it's almost always in a happy-go-lucky area; the schools are used to being visited and already have an eco-friendly environment. I have these schools and areas too, but I like to see both sides of the coin. I have been to, shall we say, 'working-class' environments where this kind of thing (meaning environmental issues and vegetarianism) is alien to them. I like that because you're really introducing something new to someone. I lived in an urban environment, and when I was young I didn't care about the environment. It meant nothing to me because it was never explained to me or linked to relevant things in my life. When some people are hesitant to speak or make cheeky comments, I have to think back to how my friends and I would react if someone spoke about this when I was at school. That means I have done work in working-class areas and schools, and middle-class areas and schools too. There are so many assumptions made about different areas. I've been to schools labelled as 'posh' and they are the most humble people you'll ever meet. The building looks fancy, but the people there are really nice. On the flipside, I've been to areas deemed as 'rough', and again people are great. This is because of stigma from the 80s and 90s carries into the twenty-first century. The Stigma I'm referring to is social baggage from the past that taints the present. Someone who lived in that time continue to brand an area without looking at the positive improvements.

These areas still carry that, and people let that stigma distort their mindset.

What I like to do is go to different cities and do work in 'working-class' and 'middle-class' areas. I can learn from both, and I get a chance to see how things work from the inside. Life is full of balance, so I want to achieve balance in different environments and reach different people. I hate to define area by class, but I prefer that than using words like 'privileged' and 'underprivileged' areas. I realise that doing this breaks down many barriers, and that's something I'm interested in doing events and activities, and allowing newspapers to show positive information about an area instead of negativity. That feels good to know that I've done something to help.

Vegetarianism vs. Vegan vs. Meat Eaters

The Vegetarian Society defines a vegetarian as: "Someone who lives on a diet of grains, pulses, nuts, seeds, vegetables and fruits with, or without, the use of dairy products and eggs. A vegetarian does not eat any meat, poultry, game, fish, shellfish or by-products of slaughter."

This means that a vegetarian is an umbrella term for different diets:

Lacto-ovo	Lacto-ovo-vegetarians eat both dairy products and eggs. This is the most common type of vegetarian diet.
Lacto	Lacto-vegetarians eat dairy products but avoid eggs.
Ovo	Ovo-vegetarians eat egg products but avoid dairy.
Vegans	Vegans avoid eating dairy products, eggs or any other products which are derived from animals.

The Vegan Society says: "A vegan is someone who tries to live without exploiting animals, for the benefit of animals, people and the planet. Vegans eat a plant-based diet, with nothing coming from animals – no meat, milk, eggs or honey, for example. A vegan lifestyle also avoids leather, wool, silk and other animal products for clothing or any other purpose."

There are many variations and interpretations when it comes to 'do not' and 'try to avoid'. I see myself as a vegetarian, but what type of vegetarian? It depends on the situation. I choose to be a raw food vegan, but if I was at a friend's house and all they had was vegetarian food then I would eat it. So I would say I'm a vegetarian who can jump between vegetarianism and veganism, a veggievegan – if that's a real word, and if not I made it up.

My View on Eating Meat

There seems to be a misconception that vegetarians/vegans don't like people who eat meat. There is some truth in that, but not from me. I grew up eating meat, and so did all my friends. It was as natural as seeing flowers in a park, nothing out of the ordinary, and there was never talk of vegetarians. I'm not in denial or ashamed of eating meat; I liked it back then. I grew up eating red meat, fish, chicken, mutton and seafood. I even joked about eating exotic food and being a daredevil eater. I made a conscious decision (in my early 20s) not to eat meat for health reasons, not necessarily for animal rights and animal welfare reasons.

I have taken a stand on animal welfare, but I shy away from the animal rights side of things. What I try and do is meet people in the middle. In my heart of hearts, I wish animals were not on the menu, but they will continue to be eaten now and for a long time after I'm not here. I would like to work towards the standards of animal care, and encourage people to lean towards local butchers and fishmongers (using all the guts) and eating local meat. Processed meat is a big problem, and using local markets and putting the money back into your city, town or village, instead of into big corporations, is a positive step forward.

No matter how strong our views are, I feel we can't completely dictate to others. It only makes people defensive and want to fire back because they feel frightened. I don't like making people feel criticised, and I don't like seeing it being done either. Only a few vegetarians and vegans actually grew up in a veggie household (based on books, articles, and conversations I've had through the years with others veggies) so I don't understand why some try so hard to break people down with their viewpoints. Some people ask me if I miss meat; is vegetarian food boring; and do I ever get tempted to eat it again? I always answer them genuinely and tell them the truth. I never miss meat; the smell doesn't make me want to eat it anymore. Seeing is believing and tasting is accepting when it comes to a plant based diet. Lastly, I don't get tempted to eat meat, but dairy products I do, and I think most vegans can admit how hard it can be to resist diary items on display in shops and bakeries. That's one of the reasons why I say I'm a vegetarian.

Why Do People Become Vegetarians and Vegans?

Another big misconception is that vegetarians and vegans think eating meat is bad, people who eat meat are bad, and they're very concerned about the rights of animals. That is completely wrong. There are people who believe that, but there are other sides too. I'm going to let you know the majority of reasons so you have clearer vision of why people take this step:

For health reasons: excessive meat eating can be linked to diseases. Most cases of food poisoning are from animal products. Factory farms (factory farming is the process of raising livestock in confinement at high stock density, where a farm operates as a business), slaughterhouses, abattoirs, meat works (a facility where animals are killed for consumption as food products), and meat packing plants can be extremely unsanitary places. In addition, meat takes a very long time to be digested.

For ethical/philosophical reasons: people believe that the meat industry is cruel to animals, and that animals should not be raised for slaughter. In addition, that we deny animals their natural rights by reducing them to meat. Some people believe it is wrong to kill and eat animals, and they don't like animals being in factory farms and in the slaughterhouses. Those animals have feelings and a personality just like us, and for this reason some people think eating meat is morally wrong.

For environmental reasons to help improve the planet: meat production can destroy and endanger the rainforests. It produces lots of methane (a greenhouse gas) and water pollution in the form of sewage. Livestock can produce more greenhouse gases than cars. Vegetarian food can use much less water. You can produce many more pounds of vegetarian food with the resources it takes to produce one pound of meat.

For political reasons: some people believe that, if resources were diverted from meat production, there could be enough food to feed everyone on the earth. Meat production can be wasteful. A fairer distribution of food and resources in the world is possible if the food fed to farm animals was used to feed people instead. Much of the food grown in the world goes to feeding livestock.

For religious reasons/spiritual advancement: some religions such as Hinduism, Buddhism, Rastafarianism and Jainism encourage people to become vegetarian. They believe eating meat creates bad karma.

For psychological reasons: some people find meat unappealing because they become aware of what they are eating and what diseases it can hold. Also, they realise how strange it is to eat a living thing. In addition, some might not like the taste of meat or dairy and opt for something else.

Now, how do you feel hearing all these explanations? So many people don't know these other options, so it's important to keep an open mind. When someone says they're a vegetarian, it could be because they just don't like the taste of meat and it has nothing to do with ethics. Thousands of articles say we, as humans, are designed to eat meat, and many others say we're meant to eat vegetables only. So, who's right? Like I always say, if you want to know something then ask. Assumptions can get you into a lot of trouble.

Stereotypes

What is a stereotype? Well, it's a fixed, over-generalized belief about a particular group or class of people. When you look at the imagery of a vegetarian (either in magazines or Google images) it's often a caucasian female holding fruit or doing yoga positions and appearing spiritual and uplifting. Vegans are seen in a different light, usually linked with animal rights. They may have dreadlocks, sandals, speaking peace and love and all that Kumbaya stuff that we expect. Being a young black male from an urban environment breaks the stereotype. I believe I'm changing things; changing views. I'm not saying I'm a revolutionary, but things have to progress in life. Vegetables and vegetarianism is usually linked with females, and meat linked with men: 'Man meat' hunter-gatherer, killing something with your hands. It's a nice depiction, I guess, but we do rely on agriculture to eat too.

There are so many vegetarian celebrities out there and you wouldn't think for a second that they were. A diet shouldn't be able to be seen by what you wear. Can you really tell if someone is a vegetarian by clothing alone? I would just like to live in a society that sees dietary beliefs like religious ones: everyone has their own beliefs. You can learn from what people do, but you don't have to feel pressured to follow it.

For this shift to happen, someone has to be the pioneer and start the ball rolling. I'm not saying I'm the face of vegetarianism, but if I become the face of vegetarianism then I won't complain. Most people I know talk but don't stand up for what they do. I do both. Talk is cheap sometimes.

You need to actually do something if you want something to change in life. Experiences can make you really gutsy and allow you to take chances and make educated decisions.

Stereotypes are in our hands. If we give in to them then they stick, but if we can become mobile then they won't be fixed, and people will see things differently.

Education

I think the key thing to improving food waste is education: talking to the food technology teachers and doing talks in schools; how to cut vegetables; what is and isn't edible; using caddy bins; talking about environmental issues and combining it with food technology. That's the way forward. I have done work in schools and I've really enjoyed it; putting myself out there and talking with young people and with the teachers; having classes that are fun, interactive and all about experimenting. Not showing people one way, but many ways and adapting to individuals' skill. I believe everyone can cook, and once the pressure of perfection is taken away, the enjoyment and achievement of being able to make simple dishes for you and others can start.

Most young people learn to cook from their parents, or from a mature member of the family (granny, et cetera). Schools teach cooking, but most cooking skills come from the home. When I was at school, cooking was quite fun, making cookies, pancakes and little cakes.

Education is really important and if you have a school willing to find the time in their curriculum to include talks, presentations and demonstrations this can be positive. Also, having a teacher who is enthusiastic and supports what you do is an added bonus. I've had some really positive experiences in schools where both the students and teachers were engaged in the session. Hopefully different people (parents or teachers) will have access to this book and see what they can do to improve schools and their pupils' knowledge. These things can't happen overnight but, in time, people can adapt themselves to new ideas.

Has My Food Gone Off?

Sometimes I feel that people have lost their sense of smell: that they are unable to sense when milk has gone off, when things are ready or should be thrown away. The key to success is passing skills and knowledge on to the next generation. The World War II generation know even more about this than me; making use of food and making it last, on a budget and making it taste nice. I have a list of foods that (if they go off or become stale) you can still use:

Bananas	Mix them into banana bread, cookies, batter, puddings and smoothies.
Bruised fruit	Cut off the bruised area and chop the rest up into a fruit salad.
Sour milk	Use it to make scones, cornbread, or another baked recipe that calls for milk or buttermilk. You can also use it to moisten pancake batter.
Pasta sauce	Freeze it in ice cube trays and use later. The trick is to freeze it before it goes bad – be honest about whether you will use the rest within three to five days!
Stale bread	Stale bread is an important ingredient in many dishes, some of which were Invented for the express purpose of using up otherwise unpalatable stale bread. Examples include: bread pudding and bread sauce.

Food Waste Tips

I think the key to reducing food waste is making a list of things to do. You should **write a list** and plan your meals for a week. Check the ingredients in your fridge and cupboards; then write a shopping list for just the extras you need. Then **stick to the list!** Take your list with you, try not to be tempted by offers, and don't shop when you're hungry.

You can ensure you **keep a healthy fridge** by checking that the seals on your fridge and the fridge temperature are good. Food needs to be stored between one and five degrees celsius for maximum freshness and longevity. And **don't throw things away!** Fruit that is just going soft can be made into smoothies, and vegetables that are starting to wilt can be made into soup. When you buy new food from the store, **rotate:** bring all the older items in your cupboards and fridge to the front. Put the new food towards the back, and you run less risk of finding something mouldy at the back of your fridge.

Be sure to **use up your leftovers** instead of scraping them into the bin – why not use them tomorrow? And **serve small amounts**, knowing that everybody can come back for more once they've cleared their plate. This is especially helpful for children whose eyes can be bigger than their stomachs. This can help reduce wasted food in caddie bins because the food would be eaten and not scraped away. The aim is the have a caddie bin of inedible food, father then edible cooked food that's been leftover.

Buy what you need. Buy loose fruit and vegetables instead of pre-packed, and then you can buy exactly the amount you need. Choose meats and cheese from a deli so that you can buy what you want. Also the bigger supermarkets have fresh meat counters too. If you only eat a small amount of bread then **freeze** it when you get home and take out a few slices a couple of hours before you need them and you can even **turn leftovers into garden food**. Some food waste is unavoidable, so why not set up a compost bin for fruit and vegetable peelings.

How Long Should I Keep This?

Shelf life is different from expiration date: this refers to food quality. A product that has passed its shelf life might still be safe, but quality is no longer guaranteed. In most food stores, waste is minimized by using something called stock rotation which involves moving products with the earliest sell by date from the warehouse to the sales area, and then to the front of the shelf, so that most shoppers will pick them up first and the products are likely to be sold before the end of their shelf life. This is important, as consumers enjoy fresher projects, plus stores can be fined for selling out of date products. For some foods, health issues are important in determining shelf life. For example, pasteurized milk can remain fresh for five days after its sell-by date if it is refrigerated properly. In contrast, if milk already has harmful bacteria, the use-by dates become irrelevant.

Best Before

Best before or best by dates appear on a wide range of frozen, dried, tinned and other foods. These dates are only advisory and refer to the quality of the product. Use by dates, indicate that the product may not be safe to consume after the specified date. Food kept after the best before date will not necessarily be harmful, but may begin to lose its preferred flavour and texture. Eggs are a special case, since they may contain salmonella which multiplies over time; they should be eaten before the best before date.

Use By

Generally, foods that have a use by date written on the packaging must not be eaten after the specified date. This is because such foods usually go bad quickly and may be harmful to someone's health. It is also important to follow storage instructions carefully for these foods (for example, some products must be refrigerated). Foods with a best before date are usually safe to eat for a time after that date, although they are likely to lack flavour, and can vary in texture, appearance, or nutritional value.

Food Storage

Food waste can be reduced in the kitchen by preserving unused or uneaten food for later use. You can preserve pantry food, such as spices, or dry ingredients, like rice and flour, for eventual use in cooking. Tupperware and other plastic storage containers can be used to store food.

Food Rotation

Food rotation is important to preserve freshness. When food is rotated, the food that has been in storage the longest is used first, and the oldest food is used as soon as possible, so that nothing is in storage too long and becomes unsafe to eat.

Every Little Helps

I think it's great when people do what they can; not to be too overwhelmed with recycling and not wasting anything, but taking mini steps and doing things gradually. This could mean having a shopping list of food that you need to buy, and checking first what you already have in your cupboard. Also, it could be scraping food waste into a caddy bin instead of a general bin. Little steps can make a big difference.

People often compliment me on my easy-going approach, because I realise doing something new is tough. New information should be given in small amounts, and any amount of effort a person makes should be appreciated.

Life can be hard and stressful, and time can disappear like quicksand. Routine and order can be so useful, and these things can really help you and your household. Some people already do these things, which is great. Others don't, and it's just about being aware of the positive aspects of doing these things. The way food waste is presented is borderline dull at times. It just doesn't seem to capture people's imagination. My aim is to change all of this: encourage people and make learning fun, make it a habit. Every little helps.

Make the Most of Leftovers

Make the most of leftovers in the following foods:

Skordalia	Skordalia is a thick puree (or sauce, dip, spread, etc.) in Greek cuisine made by combining crushed garlic with a bulky base – which may be a purée of potatoes, walnuts, almonds, or liquid-soaked stale bread – and then beating in olive oil to make a smooth emulsion. Vinegar is often added.
Garbure	Garbure is a thick French soup or stew of ham with cabbage and other vegetables, usually with cheese and stale bread added.
Fondue	Fondue is a Swiss, French, and Italian dish of melted cheese served in a communal pot over a portable stove and eaten by dipping long-stemmed forks with bread into the cheese. Stale bread is great for sopping up hot, gooey cheese, and the liquids in the fondue will soften the bread.
Croutons	A crouton is a piece of rebaked bread, often cubed and seasoned, that is used to add texture and flavour to salads (notably the Caesar salad), as an accompaniment to soups, or eaten as a snack food. Dry or stale leftover bread is usually used instead of fresh bread.
Haslet	Haslet is a pork meatloaf with herbs originally from Lincolnshire, England. Haslet is a meatloaf typically made from stale white bread, ground pork, sage, salt and black pepper. It is typically served cold

Gazpacho

with pickles and salad, or as a sandwich filling. Haslet is typically served as part of a cold meat platter, with pickles and salad, or as a sandwich filling.

Gazpacho is usually a tomato-based, vegetable soup, traditionally served cold, originating in the southern Spanish region of Andalucía. Gazpacho is widely consumed in Spanish cuisine. Gazpacho is mostly consumed during the summer months, due to its refreshing qualities and cold serving temperature. Particularly it uses stale bread, garlic, olive oil, salt and vinegar.

Wodzionka

Wodzionka is the Silesian bread or water soup made from stale bread, fat, and water. Traditionally, wodzionka is prepared by soaking two to three-day-old stale bread in water or broth and adding garlic, bay leaves, pepper and other seasonings, fried bacon, and lard or butter. It was reportedly served in late autumn and winter, when cows had less milk.

French toast

French toast, also known as eggy bread and gypsy toast, is a dish of bread soaked in beaten eggs and then fried. French toast is better with stale bread than with fresh, because stale bread will absorb more of the custard mixture than fresh bread will. Indeed, it's traditional to make French toast from day-old bread. But if all you have is fresh bread, try toasting it very slightly beforehand.

Health

Health is always linked to cooking, but what does healthy mean? External appearances cannot always be used to determine the health of a person. Just because someone is thin doesn't make them healthy, and just because someone looks overweight doesn't mean they are unhealthy. It's about how you feel; listening to your body. Salt and sugar concern me more than anything else. Food has less sugar in it now than it did years ago. The problem we have now is having access to such cheap food available twenty-four hours a day (depending on where you live). I try my best to work within the healthy template. This ranges from super healthy and pricy, super unhealthy and cheap, and a little healthy and affordable. It's a juggling act at times. Including a lot of raw food really helps, as does food that fills your stomach more and stops you snacking.

I try to eat well, on a budget and keep active. It's difficult because there are so many unhealthy snacks out there that are so cheap, but if I'm going to have one it will be one and one only. Also, it's difficult because, when you're down, you don't care what you eat.

The funniest thing is when people say, "I'm eating healthily now", and you see them eating a salad and an apple. You can eat healthily without eating salad and apples all day. All these articles telling you what you should and shouldn't eat can be confusing. Even for me, I hear one thing and then a conflicting thing afterwards. From what I know, let me give you an outline of healthy food:

Vegetables

Asparagus
Avocados
Beetroots
Bell pepper
Broccoli
Brussels sprouts
Cabbage
Carrots
Cauliflower
Celery

Collard greens
Cucumbers
Aubergine/eggplant
Fennel
Garlic
Green beans
Green peas
Kale
Leeks
Mushrooms
Olives
Onions
Potatoes
Romaine lettuce
Sea vegetables
Spinach
Squash, summer
Squash, winter
Sweet potatoes
Swiss chard
Tomatoes
Turnip greens
Yams

Seafood

Cod
Halibut
Salmon
Sardines
Scallops
Shrimp
Tuna

Fruits

Apples
Apricots
Bananas
Blueberries

Cantaloupe
Cranberries
Figs
Grapefruit
Grapes
Kiwi fruit
Lemons/limes
Oranges
Papaya
Pears
Pineapple
Plums
Prunes
Raisins
Raspberries
Strawberries
Watermelon

Eggs and low-fat dairy

Cheese
Eggs
Milk: semi skimmed milk, goat's milk, soya milk, almond milk, hazelnut milk, rice milk, oat milk and coconut milk
Yogurt

Beans and legumes

Black beans
Dried peas
Chickpeas
Kidney beans
Lentils
Lima beans
Miso
Broad beans
Pinto beans
Soybeans
Tofu and tempeh

Poultry and lean meats

Beef, lean organic
Chicken
Lamb
Turkey
Venison

Nuts, seeds and oils

Almonds
Cashews
Flaxseeds
Olive oil, extra virgin
Peanuts
Pumpkin seeds
Sesame seeds
Sunflower seeds
Walnuts

Grains

Barley
Brown rice
Buckwheat
Corn
Millet
Oats
Quinoa
Rye
Spelt
Wholewheat

Spices and herbs

Basil
Black pepper
Cayenne pepper
Chilli pepper, dried
Coriander seeds
Cinnamon, ground
Cloves
Cumin seeds
Dill
Ginger
Mustard seeds
Oregano
Parsley
Peppermint
Rosemary
Sage
Thyme
Turmeric

Natural sweeteners

Blackstrap molasses
Honey
Maple syrup

Other

Green tea
Soy sauce
Water

From my independent research, these are the approved things that are healthy. The foods on the list have a high-level nutritional value. Also, they are whole foods and have not been highly processed. These foods are familiar because they are common everyday Western food. In addition, local supermarkets stock all these foods. The food is affordable and not overpriced unless it's organic. (Organic products take more people power to produce so it's more expensive, and takes longer to produce because its not aided by chemical enhancers.) Lastly, they taste good and can be used for many different recipes. Now, how you use these vegetables is a different story.

Is There Such a Thing As Junk Food?

What is junk food? We use this phrase all the time but we never really investigate what means. For example, people say chips are bad for children, but I believe they're wrong. What makes something a chip? The shape, the fact that it's a potato or that it's fried?

Alow me to further explain this: potatoes are still vegetables and have a place in well-rounded diet, even when they are made into fabulous French fries. Potatoes contain more potassium than banana and are packed with half a daily serving of vitamin C and as much protein as a cup of milk. No matter what you do with them, potatoes are a solid foundation for a healthy side dish.

With such a healthy starting point, it is easy to make French fries that everyone will love without stripping them of their nutritional content or adding things that change a tasty treat into an unhealthy one. Start by keeping those nutrient rich skins on the potatoes. You can slice and dice them in whatever way you want; just don't peel them first.

One way to make a healthier French fry is to bake them in the oven. Start with your sliced potatoes, put them in a plastic bag, with a drizzle of olive oil to coat the fries; then toss them in your favourite seasoning before spreading them out on a cookie sheet. The key to crispness is making sure they are spread out enough so they aren't touching each other and have space to cook properly.

Another way to make great fries is to cook them on the grill. Place the cookie sheet under the hot grill. Turn a few times to keep the fries from sticking and soon you have a delicious accompaniment to your hot dogs and hamburger. This method also works great with store-bought fries that are meant to be cooked in the oven. Make sure you check the nutrition label and pick a brand without trans-fat and with the lowest saturated fat and sodium totals.

Although it is often the act of frying that gets French fries on the 'worst dressed' list, you can still achieve that deep-fried texture and flavour without sacrificing your health. Instead of immersing fries in a vat of oil, coat a pan with a tablespoon or two of olive oil and fry them up in frying pan. Add your favourite seasoning to spice things up and get ready for everyone to be amazed at how deliciously healthy French fries can be.

I Can't Cook…

"I can't cook," people say, but what does that mean? The definition of cooking is: preparing food with heat or fire. Everyone can technically 'cook' but then there's what you call 'real cooking'. Making something is easy now thanks to readymade pasta, pastry and noodles. Whether you start with making one thing from scratch a day, it's something, and hopefully it can boost your confidence and you can make something else.

Pies	Readymade pastry, and a filling.
Pasties	Readymade puff pastry and filling.
Pizzas	Readymade pizza base and topping.

These are just examples of making something quick and easy; a combination of buying and making things. You don't have to make pastry and dough to make a pizza but, whether you do or not, it's still a step towards confidence in the kitchen.

The biggest problem, which I have noticed, is the kitchen itself. Think about it: there are hobs, an oven, fridge and sink, and microwave too – but I don't see that as a 'real' piece of equipment. Most people use the fridge and microwave, but the other things are neglected. What temperature should I have the oven on? What are all these numbers? How do I turn the oven on in the first place? These are all little dilemmas that surface when cooking is presented to some people. The same way some musicians don't know how to write music or know what note is a major or minor is the same way some cooks don't have a clue about temperatures and weighing. They just know that what they do works, and that was my way at the beginning. Slowly, you learn the basics, and then if you want to go further you can. I don't see myself as any expert, more of a generalist. I would rather be OK and know the basics of fifty things than be the best in the world at one thing. I guess you can call me a jack of all trades.

Instead of saying "I can't cook" why not give it a go and let someone else be the judge? Feedback is important, but not criticism. Having someone say that they like your food can be a great confidence boost to make something more adventurous. Listen, as long as someone likes what you've made (smell and taste), and eats your meal with a smile you *can* cook. Remember that.

Cooking Equipment

When you think cooking, you imagine equipment, and some might fear they don't have the right equipment. Really, all you need are the basics. You don't need fancy pans, special, expensive equipment or things like that. You should be able to manage with the following:

Saucepans	A small saucepan is great for boiling vegetables, eggs, potatoes. A larger one is useful if you are going to cook a soup or a huge stew for a large group.
Measuring jug	Invaluable. A large plastic measuring jug is not only useful for measuring liquids such as water and stock, but can also be used as an impromptu mixing bowl.
Frying pan	Great for everything: pancakes and omelettes, full English breakfast and all fried dishes.
Colander	Brilliant for draining water from pasta, rice, potatoes, vegetables. The list is endless. Plastic and metal versions work equally well.
Wok	Quick for stir-fry meals.
Sieve	Don't really need, but just in case for baking.
Mixing bowl	Use it for melting chocolate, cake mixing, making pesto, home-made burgers, and whipping up swift salad dressings.
Blender	Great for soups, smoothies and cocktails.
Potato masher	Good for mashing potatoes and vegetables such as butternut squash and carrots.
Vegetable peeler	Great for peeling vegetables and fruit.
Can opener	Opens cans of beans, tuna, coconut milk, canned tomatoes and everything that is canned.

Grater	For grating cheese, and also great for grating garlic and ginger.
Whisk	Even though you can whisk eggs fairly well with a fork, a whisk is very handy when making omelettes as it gives them a lovely light texture. Also handy for whisking cream or egg whites.
Spatula	A plastic spatula is a great implement for scraping up all the leftovers from a mixing bowl. A metal version is useful when you need to lift and drain fried food, such as when cooking a breakfast fry-up.
Wooden spoon	Used for baking or stirring soups.
Small knives	To cut fruits, vegetables or anything else.
Large knives	Can be used to cut meat, herbs, vegetables or fruit.

Different Ways to Cook

There are many methods of cooking, most of which have been known since antiquity. These include baking, roasting, frying, grilling, barbecuing, smoking, boiling, steaming and braising. A more recent innovation is microwaving. Various methods use differing levels of heat and moisture, and vary in cooking time. The method chosen greatly affects the end result. Some foods are more appropriate to some methods than others. Some cooking techniques include:

Baking	Besides breads and desserts, you can bake seafood, poultry, lean meat, vegetables and fruits. For baking, place food in a pan or dish surrounded by the hot, dry air of your oven. You may cook the food covered or uncovered. Baking generally doesn't require that you add fat to the food.
Braising	Braising involves browning the ingredient first in a pan on top of the stove, and then slowly cooking it covered with a small quantity of liquid, such as water or broth. In some recipes, the cooking liquid is used afterwards to form a flavourful, nutrient-rich sauce.

Broiling/grilling	Both broiling and grilling expose food to direct heat. To grill outdoors, place the food on a grill rack above a bed of charcoal embers or gas-heated rocks. If you have an indoor grill, follow the manufacturer's directions. For smaller items such as chopped vegetables, use foil or a long-handled grill basket to prevent pieces from slipping through the rack. To broil indoors, place the food on a broiler rack below a heat element. Both methods allow fat to drip away from the food.
Poaching	Poaching is the process of gently simmering food in liquid, generally milk, stock or wine.
Roasting	Roasting is a cooking method that uses dry heat, whether an open flame, oven, or other heat source.
Sautéing	Sautéing is a method of cooking food that uses a small amount of oil or fat in a shallow pan over relatively high heat.
Steaming	Steaming is a method of cooking using steam. Steaming is considered a healthy cooking technique and capable of cooking almost all kinds of food.
Stir-frying	Frying is the cooking of food in oil or another fat.
Smoking	Smoking is the process of flavouring, cooking, or preserving food by exposing it to the smoke from burning or smouldering plant materials, most often wood. Meats and fish are the most common smoked foods.

Other methods of cooking include: barbecuing, rotisserie, searing, baking blind, flashbaking, blanching, coddling, double steaming, infusion, pressure cooking, simmering, smothering, steeping, stewing, vacuum flask cooking, deep frying, hot salt frying, hot sand frying, pan frying, and pressure frying. Never allow anyone to tell you what you need to cook a meal. There are so many different ways to make bread, make cakes and prepare things based on your culture, and chefs and other cooks only have an opinion. I'll tell you about a conversation that I had with a Chinese guy I met. We were discussing food and he was stunned how many different pots and pans there were in an English kitchen. He said that everyone in China used a pan, wok or a steamer. He found kitchens with an oven, microwave and hobs fascinating. So I asked him, "If you don't use ovens then how do you make bread?" He said he used a steamer to make Chinese bread called mantou. Now, the funny thing about this story was that when I said 'bread', I picture traditional white bread from a bakery. In his mind, bread is steamed and circular. I couldn't imagine that bread could be boiled; just oven-baked because that's what had been fed to me in imagery from films, adverts and books. It was interesting because all he needed was heat (a flame), one pot, one wok and one steamer. That's three pieces of equipment for basically everything. But, in a typically Western kitchen, you need one pot for this, one pot for that, an oven for this, et cetera. I've since learnt that the key to cooking is being versatile, and opening my mind to different methods.

Raw food involves eating food that hasn't been cooked, so cooking equipment isn't needed. You don't need heat so you don't need electrical appliances – foraging and eating food in its natural state. Meeting different people gives you a different perspective. Not every kitchen is the same, so never let equipment scare you from cooking.

Presentation

Presentation is the key thing when it comes to food. Presentation first; then taste. Or smell, presentation and then taste. You can make standard food look fancy, and fancy, expensive food look cheap. Presentation is the key to a good meal. The problem nowadays is 'food perfection'. Like people, food has to look perfect and attractive in every aspect. If people can't duplicate how a pie looks in their recipe then they see it as a failure and become discouraged. I always say I can make any ordinary meal look fancy. It's always about presentation and the way you set the plate. Whether its beans and toast, spaghetti on toast or a simple sandwich, the way it looks is important.

When I started to create my recipes, I decided to take professional pictures of my food. I know the visual is more important than just the name, but the name also helps too. A name that stays in your head is always good.

An important thing is making things look neat, wiping the plate so there are no spillages, and having a little napkin folded by the plate. It's the little things that help make a meal great, so looks definitely do matter.

I always say to people I can make any regular meal look posh with the right presentation.

Food Perfection

I think the word 'perfect' should never be used with food. I believe there isn't a perfect cake, or a perfect pizza. We all have opinions, and we will all have a different view on what's great. People might want tomatoes to look firm, red and curvaceous, yet does it matter if we're going to cut it anyway? Should we eat it or just look at it? I love food presentation, but food can look so polished that it should be in a museum or frozen to contain the beauty. It's just a strange world we live in now. Some recipe books can be a turn-off because of the intimidating professional pictures taken. I believe there are some pictures that look so perfect that by mere sight it can hold someone back from even attempting make the recipe. So who's in the wrong and who's in the right?

Wonky food is ignored, and fruit and vegetables with the right look are picked. I'm not going to lie: this food looks visually great, but does it taste better? Once its cut, does it really matter? We're in a position where we can pick and choose, but in many places in the world there is no choice. If rice or bread is part of your staple diet, and food is grown and looks a little strange, then that's what you're going to eat.

It's funny because I don't think people realise what is done to food to make it look so great in the picture. Not everyone uses these techniques (I certainly don't), but just so you know:

Blowtorch	For browning the edges of raw burgers and the goose-bumpy skins of nearly raw poultry.
Cotton balls	Which, when soaked and microwaved, perform quite nicely in creating the illusion of steaming hot foods.
Spray deodorant	Which gives grapes a desirable veneer.
Hairspray	Which can give the appearance of new life to a dried out piece of cake.
Toothpicks	To hold sandwiches together.
Tweezers	For looping noodles in the stir fry and rearranging miniscule yet crucial crumbs.
Brown shoe polish	So raw meat appears succulent and roasted.

White glue	Used instead of milk for cereal photos.
Spraying food	With water or mixtures of water, corn syrup or other liquids to keep food looking fresh.
Heavy cream	Instead of milk in bowls of cereal to stop flakes from becoming too soggy quickly.

FOOD WASTE RECIPES

Pizza Crostini
Serves 1

Ingredients
1 slice of bread
Tomato purée
A couple of slices of cucumber
A slice of tomato
Mozzarella cheese (cheddar would work too)
Yellow and red pepper
Sea salt, black pepper, sunflower oil

Instructions
Toast a slice of bread (stale bread is fine). Cut into circles with a cup and blitz the rest into breadcrumbs which you can freeze in a bag for another time, (to use as a topping with cheese for a veggie bake). Spread some tomato purée on the bread. Add however much grated mozzarella cheese you want, chopped yellow and red peppers, slice of tomato, sea salt and black pepper. Add a splash of sunflower oil and put in the oven at 180C/350F/Gas Mark 4 for a couple of minutes (keep checking to make sure it doesn't burn). Top with a slice of cucumber and eat!

Tudor Salad
Serves 1

Ingredients

A couple of handfuls of baby leaf salad
1 slice of bread
A few chunks of cucumber
Kalamata and green olives (optional)
A few chunks of feta cheese
Dash of olive oil
Parsley and chives

Instructions

Add salad leaves to your plate. Cut the slice of bread into mini squares (croutons), and fry in olive oil. Cut the kalamata and green olives in half. Cut the feta cheese into mini squares. Dress with olive oil, parsley and chives.

Mediterranean Spicy Omelette
Serves 1

Ingredients
3 eggs (with yolk)
Finely chopped yellow and red peppers
Grated mozzarella cheese
Mushrooms
Sunflower oil
Mixed herbs (basil, thyme, marjoram,
oregano, sage and parsley)
Sea salt and black pepper corns

Instructions
Whisk all the ingredients in a bowl for
5 minutes. Add mixture to a hot pan of
oil until cooked on both sides.

Banana Skin Curry
Serves 2

Ingredients

1 whole leek

2 red onions

2 white onions

1 red pepper

1 green pepper

1 yellow pepper

5 mushrooms

1–2 banana skins

Italian seasoning (sesame seeds, sea salt, basil, parsley, oregano, garlic granules, thyme, ground black pepper and sage)

Chives

Parsley

Turmeric

Curry powder

Agave syrup

Instructions

Cut all the vegetables up as finely as possible and toss into a bowl. Season the vegetables. Add 3 tsp of each herb and spice and mix it all around with a spoon. Get a frying pan or wok, put some olive oil in it and fry the vegetables – make sure everything is soft, especially the peppers. Get a bowl and put the banana skin (whole) in there with hot water for 12 minutes. Make sure the banana skins are soft. Test one by eating a small piece to see if it's soft. Once cooked, drain them, cut the black ends off the bananas and cut them up into little pieces. Add them to the pan of mixed vegetables, add some sea salt, black pepper and agave syrup, and add 3 tbsp of each spice and herb again. Once everything is fried, leave it to cook down more and then serve with rice flavoured with chives, parsley, sea salt and black pepper.

Bread Batons With Thai Chilli Sauce
Serves 1

Ingredients

Bread crusts from 2 slices of bread
1 egg
200g self-raising flour
Mixed herbs (basil, thyme, marjoram, oregano, sage and parsley)
Salt and pepper to taste
450ml water

Instructions

Put self-raising flour into a bowl with the rest of the ingredients. Mix until it resembles a batter. Put the crusts from the bread into the mixture and fry in a pan until brown. Garnish with sweet Thai chilli sauce.

Spanish Cheese on Toast
Serves 1

Ingredients
White bread
Kalamata and green olives
Feta cheese
1 Tomato
Maple syrup

Instructions
Toast the bread. Add the feta cheese (to taste). Cut the kalamata and green olives up and scatter over. Slice or chop the tomato and put on top of the cheese. Add a drizzle of maple syrup on top and grill until all has melted.

Sweet French Domitille
Serves 1

Ingredients

1 slice of white bread

A squirt of maple syrup (golden syrup will also work)

A knob of butter (dairy-free butter if needing it to be vegan)

A few strawberries

Instructions

Toast a slice of white bread. Cut diagonally and put in a frying pan with the butter. Add maple or golden syrup to the toast on both sides. Add strawberries and fry until they have glazed with the syrup.

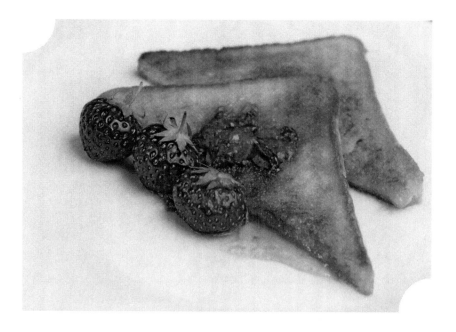

Curried Pancakes
Serves 2 – 4

Ingredients
280g gram flour
2 tbsp vegetable oil
200ml water
2tbsp curry powder
100g mixed vegetables finely chopped
(e.g. courgette and tomato)

Instructions
Stir the gram flour and curry powder in a large mixing bowl. Gradually add the water and mix with a hand blender to form a smooth batter. Mix in the vegetables. Heat the oil in a frying pan and spoon in one ladle of the batter. Fry on one side for a minute or two then cook the other side by flipping with a spatula. Serve when pancakes are lightly browned.

Winter Wicca Pie
Serves 4 – 6

Ingredients

2 large carrots
2 large parsnips
2 large leeks (chopped finely)
3 cloves of minced garlic
2 shallots
1 tablespoon of parsley
1 tablespoon of chives
2 pinches of black pepper
2 pinches of sea salt
3 cloves of minced or chopped garlic
5 tablespoons of vegetable powder
6 tablespoons of tomato purée
Readymade shortcrust pastry
(preferably wholemeal)

Instructions

Chop mixed vegetables. Put the vegetables (carrots, parsnips, leeks and shallots) in a medium-sized pot filled with boiling hot water, the water just covering the vegetables. Add vegetable power and tomato purée to the water. Then add parsley, chives, black pepper, salt and garlic. Reduce the heat and simmer gently for an hour and a half. Preheat the oven to 190C/375F/Gas 5. Transfer the filling mixture to a dish, line the rim of the dish with a thin strip of pastry (wholemeal is best and the healthier option). Dampen the pastry rim by brushing it with warmed butter. Cut a piece of pastry to fit across the top of the dish and place on top of the dish, pressing the edges together to seal it. Decorate with pastry trimmings. Make a steam hole in the centre of the pie by slashing with a sharp knife. Then brush with more melted butter. Transfer the dish to the oven and cook for 1–1½ hours. Keep checking the oven until the pastry is brown. Serve hot or cold.

Child's Play

No one loves cooking (or pretending to cook) like children. Be in a child's setting, bringing play dough out and seeing the reaction – there's a lot of excitement. When I was young, I loved play dough. Even now, I enjoy it (while in a childcare setting working with children) and children enjoy it too. Having playdough helps because it's like cooking dough, or flour. Short crust, sweet crust and bread dough resemble that type of look and texture. Having this easy experience is so important for children's development, and cooking skills later in life. You can make play dough easily, and if not you can buy toy food. Toy food is so realistic, so children can use pots and pans and play kitchen with the pretend food.

Play dough is a classic childhood toy everyone can have fun with, and it's so easy to make at home you'll never buy that stinky store variety again.

An easy play dough recipe is: 1 cup flour, 1 cup water, 1/2 cup salt, 1 tablespoon vegetable oil, 1 tablespoon cream of tartar (optional for improved elasticity), food colouring (liquid, powder or unsweetened drink mix), scented oils.

In addition, using cookie/biscuit cutters is great. They come in so many different shapes and sizes: circles, squares, hands, feet, teddy bears and everything under the sun. Picture shapes mixed with colours make play dough a fun experience for children and adults. These are just tips that can help children develop, give them something to do and give them the experience of cooking in their mind.

I have designed certain recipes with children in mind. In particular, my coconut island cakes that use natural ingredients. They're simple to make and look pretty.

Coconut Island Cakes

Ingredients

2 tsp coconut oil

Agave nectar or maple syrup

5 handful of desiccated (shreddded) coconut

1 handful of dried apricots

Instructions

Place all of the ingredients into a food processor and add the maple syrup until it is all mixed together. If you are able to make a solid ball from the mixture then it is ready; if it doesn't stick together then add more maple syrup. Make little balls from the mixture, place on a plate and put them in the fridge for 20 minutes. After 20 minutes take out of the fridge and eat for a sweet healthy snack. These things are designed to build the adult-child relationship and make the activity fun and enjoyable.

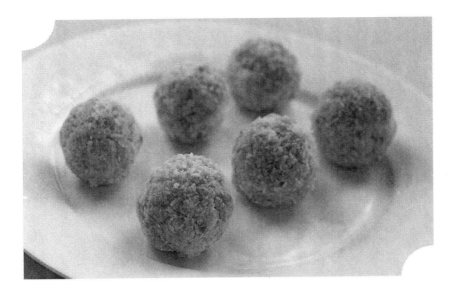

Final Thoughts

Well, the book is almost done. All my final thoughts said, and I hope you have got something from this book. I've said everything I could possibly say about food, food waste and cooking. I haven't said everything about myself because I had to stick to the cooking side of Shane Jordan, but I hope it was an enjoyable read. More than anything, I hope it's a book you can look through again and find certain parts useful. Also, that you can pass it on to a friend or recommend it as a thought-provoking book.

Lastly, people ask me why I do what I do. It's a good question. This took me a long time to think about: looking at what I've done, and what I want to do in the future. The key thing is that I'm passionate about something. Passion meaning I have a deep desire to do something that fills my body with positive, warm, nice feelings. So I like to cook and create, and have freedom and learn new things. Now, mix that with motivation for a cause that you feel passionate about with a mission. I see food waste as a problem, and there is a solution. It's basic in form, but doing it takes people and change. I like people to be a part of the solution, not the problem. It's not about winning or losing, just taking part.

What started off as cooking fun moved into vegetarianism, cooking, food waste, then food education, cooking skills, education, and cooking on a therapeutic level. Food is bigger than I thought, and still may touch on deeper levels than I know now in times to come. I just want to see how far I can go with food, do my part and hopefully encourage others to pursue things that they are passionate about. I'm no role model; just someone who is tired of seeing things and waiting for people to do something. I do other things apart from cooking, but this is a part of my life that I'm pursuing more than anything else. I see myself as a jack of all trades, forever busy doing different things. In life, we have the chance to pursue what we want. What stops us is ourselves. It's not easy to stand amongst people and do something different. Confidence, ability and creativity can go further than you think. The more events and experiences I have with food, sustainability and environmental issues, the more these qualities are increased. I would like to be known as someone who did something different, and changed something. It doesn't have to be big, but just something little. I would be happy and content with that. It's great to have support from close supporters, editors of magazines and newspapers, organisations and the public.

There's no one doing what I'm doing right now, but I hope others can seen what I'm doing and see what I've done, and follow what they believe in or assist with the project. People say to me, "You're famous now", and I shy away from that and say, "No." It's not about being famous; it's about being useful. It's nice to be able to do something (paid or voluntary) that makes use of your skills. The saddest thing is for someone to have skills and abilities in something and not share them. It's all about sharing skills and talents, and hopefully from that will spout creativity. It's not about being the best; just being able to do something on a basic level. I see everything that I do as a progression. I can always improve on something, so that always keeps me humble and grounded. People have so many skills but they fail to see it because others put you down, or don't see your full potential. Whatever you're able to do to help or bring a smile to someone's face can be nurtured and grown into a hobby, and maybe a career. I'm not trying to be a role model, or a great inspiring figure. Just someone who has used their skills, had an idea about combating a problem, and has found a solution that's fun and enjoyable.

The key thing is being conscious in life: being aware of things and asking yourself if you're comfortable with it. If I compile lots of waste and that increases the tax I have to pay (and I'm conscious of it), should I still not recycle? If I see how things are prepared in food, am I comfortable with still eating it? All these things equate to being conscious of things.

The Future of Food

I have no idea what the future of food is, but I am a little concerned about the basic culinary skills passed on by one generation to the other. With everything you can think of, people either warm up (microwave), eat on the go (food delivery), or watch someone else making food. Everyone knows there's a lot of elitism in food: people making simple recipes complicated and out of the general person's reach; having to have cooking skills from a cookery school, and have fancy equipment. I am trying to show people that you only need a recipe to give you a rough idea how to make something.

You don't need special cooking equipment.

In my opinion, the way forward is to first make cooking fun, easy, relevant and seen. No one wants to do something which isn't fun, so cooking shouldn't be a boring experience. If cooking skills become relevant then people will want to be able to do it. Having nothing to eat in the freezer one day, and having some flour to make dumplings for yourself and friends is useful and relevant for that period, and many to come. What I mean by 'seen' is that people can 'see' people cooking a lot around them, whether they're at home or at school or events. Easy, quick and tasty recipes are a great start to doing lots of things. No one has to cook every day (Monday to Sunday), but just knowing you can and doing it twice a week is something.

Bibliography

Low, C. (2006) *Platform: Why There's Still a Case For Special Treatment* [online] Available at: http://tesco.co.uk (accessed 15th February 2006)

Teacher (2006) [online] Available at: http://www.teachersnet.gov.uk (accessed 15th February 2006)

Mclveganway (2003) "The Movement for Compassionate Living" [online] Available at: http://www.mclveganway.org.uk/kathleen_jannaway.html (accessed 1st January 2013)

The Vegan Society (unknown date) [online] Available at: http://www.vegansociety.com/hubpage.aspx?id=495 (accessed 20th March 2013)

The Vegetarian Society (unknown date) [online] Available at: https://www.vegsoc.org/definition (accessed 20th March 2013)

Acknowledgements

A big thank you these people and organisations:

Arc Café
Café Kino
Charlotte Stone (front cover photographer)
Easton Community Centre
Flavour Magazine
Foodcycle
Jenny & Ian (ExcelArt)
Kabele Café
Kerry McCarthy
Miele Passmore
Natural Balance Foods
SilverWood Books
The Bristol Pigeon
The Evening Post
The Independent Newspaper
The Spark
Tim Barford
Vegan Views
Vegan Society
Vegetarian Society
Vegfest

To find out more about Shane Jordan and his work visit
www.foodwastephilosophy.com